Practical WordStar Uses

Practical WordStar™ Uses

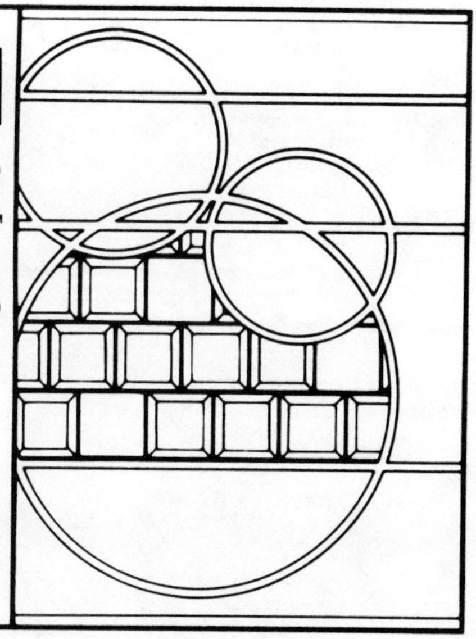

Julie Anne Arca

Berkeley • Paris • Düsseldorf SYBEX®

Cover art by Daniel Le Noury
Cartoons by Gar Smith
Design and illustrations by Gaynelle B. Grover

WordStar, MailMerge, SpellStar, DataStar, InfoStar, and SuperSort are trademarks of MicroPro International.
Apple II is a registered trademark of Apple Computer, Inc.
CP/M is a registered trademark of Digital Research, Inc.
Documate/Plus is a registered trademark of Orthocode Corp.
IBM is a trademark of International Business Machines.
Spellguard is a trademark of Innovative Software.
Proofreader and Grammatik are trademarks of Aspen Software.
Corrector is a trademark of SuperSoft.
Random House Electronic Thesaurus is a trademark of Doctronics.
Bibliography and Footnote are trademarks of Digital Marketing.
Sybex is not affiliated with any manufacturer.

Library of Congress Card Number: 83-72250
ISBN 0-89588-107-1
Printed in the United States of America
10 9 8 7 6

To Diana Doherty, (Mr.) Bob Rose, and Larry Sturhahn,
the customers who showed me how to teach them the wonders of WordStar.

Acknowledgements

Special thanks to Sybex for assistance, especially to Michael McGrath for his emotional and gastronomic support (particularly the gastronomic support), to Barbara Gordon and Joyce Cox for their thoughtful and professional editing; and to Joel Kreisman for technical review.

Thanks, too, to Wendy Mitchell of MicroPro International, who went out of her way to provide software and information so that this book would be as accurate and up-to-date as is possible in this mercurial industry.

Bob Hubar also deserves thanks for giving me the idea for ESCAPE. May he be the first to travel with them.

Very special thanks to Richard Lindstrom for his patience, tolerance, and other Boy Scout qualities that kept him from strangling me while I spent far too long finishing this book. Also thanks to him for some of the preliminary cartoon drawings.

Table of Contents

PART ONE

An Overview of WordStar

APPENDICES

Introduction

WHY YOU SHOULD READ THIS BOOK

There's a little something for everyone in this book.

If you are a WordStar beginner, it will guide you through the first confusing weeks, helping you to get to know the program and to develop useful word-processing applications.

If you are a competent intermediate operator who is comfortable with WordStar but eager to explore its power further, this book will suggest new ways of using the program.

Finally, if you are a WordStar expert, we challenge you to try to improve on the techniques suggested, or, using this book as a starting point, to develop even more exciting applications that will make WordStar an increasingly useful program for you.

In addition, if you are an office or word-processing manager or training coordinator, this book will help you develop standard word-processing forms and procedures, and will provide a useful guide for training new word-processing operators.

WHAT THIS BOOK IS ABOUT

This book is about getting the most out of your WordStar word-processing program.

Part One gives you an overview of the CP/M operating system and of WordStar. First we will show you how to get past the disk operating system—what it is, why it is important, and what a word-processing operator needs to know about it. Next, we will explain how WordStar is put together—what you need to do to get WordStar up and running and how WordStar handles files. Then we will take a brief look at the WordStar function menus and dot commands.

After this brief introduction, *Part Two* and *Part Three* are designed as a workbook of step-by-step instructions that show you how to develop and use common word-processing applications. You will learn how to create form letters, form documents, and fancy printed formats. In other words, you will learn how to get the most out of WordStar by using some of its sophisticated shortcuts.

Each of the 11 WordStar application exercises in *Part Two* includes a description of the application, suggested uses, an overview of the process, a summary of important commands, step-by-step development instructions, and a review of the process.

When you have mastered all that, in *Part Three* you will learn how to increase your productivity even more by using WordStar in cooperation with MailMerge, a set of commands that allows you to combine information stored in two different files automatically. We will explain the commands and how to insert them in WordStar files, and show you five useful and time-saving MailMerge applications.

In addition, this book contains several helpful appendices, including a summary of important WordStar commands, detailed instructions for using common CP/M and IBM PC-DOS commands, and a review of other programs that can enhance WordStar's operation.

WHICH VERSION OF WORDSTAR DO YOU HAVE?

This book was developed using features available in WordStar Version 3.0. Except for the hyphen-help and column-move features, which are not included in versions prior to Version 2.0, the features used are available in all versions of WordStar.

In June, 1983, MicroPro (WordStar's publisher) introduced WordStar Version 3.3. Basically Versions 3.0 and 3.3 offer the same capabilities, so those of you who purchase Version 3.3 will find this book just as useful as those of us who have owned the program for a while. However, Version 3.3 does include a few changes: the no-file menu is now called the opening menu, and you may use the INSTALL program to assign command functions to specific function keys on your computer's keyboard. (This procedure is not discussed in this book. Consult the Version 3.3 manual if you want to take advantage of this facility.)

The version number of your copy of WordStar should be noted on the label of your original disk. If you do not own the current version, you might want to contact your dealer or MicroPro, to find out how to update your copy of the program.

For *Part Three*, we used MailMerge Version 3.0.

HOW YOU CAN USE THIS BOOK

Of course, you can start at the beginning and read through to the end, becoming familiar with WordStar along the way. You can also skim through the book until you find specific operational or application problems that you have been trying to solve. Following are some guidelines that may help you decide how you can use this book most effectively.

What to Do before You Begin

When you purchased WordStar, you received a WordStar training manual, a WordStar reference manual, and a floppy disk or two containing all the files you need to use the program.

Before you begin to read this book, read MicroPro's WordStar training manual, which takes you step by step through all the basic WordStar functions and gives you a good outline of the program's capabilities. Then read this book. It reviews and colors in that outline, providing useful techniques for putting all WordStar's commands together to create many types of documents.

The WordStar reference manual includes everything you would ever want to know about WordStar. It may be overwhelming for a new user. Read it in small doses, as you work through MicroPro's training manual. Or put it on a shelf and read it after you have a couple of hours of training under your belt. It will make a lot more sense to you then, because it offers lots of interesting and useful information to an experienced user.

To augment the MicroPro training and reference manuals, you might consider adding *Introduction to WordStar*, written by Arthur Naiman and published by Sybex, to your word-processing library.

Which Parts of This Book Should You Read?

This book is designed so you can use it whichever way makes the most sense for you, depending on your level of expertise. Each of the three sections in *Part One* begins by describing the information that will be discussed, and explains why it is important for the WordStar operator. Read the chapter description to determine whether you are interested in or need to read that section.

At the end of each of these three sections, a summary called *What You Should Know by Now* reviews the material just presented. After reading the introduction, if you are still not sure whether you should read the whole section, quickly review the summary to make sure you already understand that material.

If you have had some exposure to WordStar, you may want to jump right into the application sections. We start with relatively simple applications and move on to progressively more complex ones, with MailMerge following WordStar, so that you become more comfortable with the program as you work through each exercise. Of course, you are welcome to start with any application. At the beginning of each exercise, you will find a description of the application that will help you decide whether you are interested in trying it.

INSTRUCTION SYMBOLS USED IN THIS BOOK

You will use a few special keys found on your computer keyboard to give commands to WordStar. To make this book as easy to understand as possible, we use three symbols that will signal you to enter information on the keyboard using specified procedures. They are intended to help you concentrate on using the applications presented in this book, without becoming bogged down by explanatory information.

The CONTROL Key

The control key on your computer keyboard may be marked CONTROL, CNTRL, or CTRL. It is depressed simultaneously with another key to signal to the computer that you want it to perform a special function, such as delete an extra letter from a word you have typed.

As you learn WordStar, you will discover that you must use many control-key commands to tell WordStar how you want to edit your documents. In both its documentation and its video displays, WordStar uses the symbol ^ to represent the control key. When we mention a control-key command within the text of this book, we will use the same symbol to let you know that you must hold down the control key and simultaneously press a letter key to give a command. For example, the command ^S moves the cursor left one character.

Hold down the control key, and press the S key simultaneously to use the command ^ S.

Because WordStar includes so many different commands, you sometimes have to press the control key and two letter keys to give a command to the program. You do not have to continue holding down the control key while pressing the second letter key, but if you do so accidentally or out of habit, WordStar still understands what you mean. For example, the command ^ KB marks the beginning of a block of text. Hold down the control key and simultaneously press the K key, then release both keys. Then press and release the B key. You will see that the result is the same as when you press the control key, the K key, and the B key all at once.

If you have used WordStar at all, you should already be comfortable using the control key to send commands to the program.

The ESCAPE Key

The escape key is generally marked ESC. In WordStar you use this key to get you out of situations you don't want to be in. Suppose you accidentally commanded WordStar to print a file when you really wanted to edit it. Press the escape key to tell WordStar you made a mistake and want to abort (escape from) the print command sequence and start over. Generally, you do not need to press any other key to make this key work for you.

Sometimes you will see (Press ESC.) in the exercises. When you read this, press and release the escape key.

The RETURN/ENTER Key

The return/enter key, conveniently enough, is generally labeled either RETURN or ENTER. On some keyboards, such as the IBM Personal Computer keyboard, there is a funny-looking arrow (↵) marking that key. However it may be marked, this key performs two different functions within a word-processing program.

When you press the return/enter key after typing a command, it operates like the transmit/receive button on a two-way radio. When you say *Over* and release the transmit button on a radio, the person listening knows you have finished transmitting and that it is his turn to transmit. When you press the return/enter key after typing a computer command, you signal to the computer that you have finished typing the command. Now it is the computer's turn to act.

In some programs, including WordStar, the return/enter key also serves the same purpose as a carriage-return key on a typewriter. When you press the carriage-return key on a typewriter, the paper is moved up one line and the print element is moved to the left margin. You are then ready to type a new line or paragraph. In computerized word processing, you press the return/enter key not at the end of each line but at the end of each paragraph. In response, the computer moves the cursor down to the left margin of the next line so that you can begin a new paragraph.

When you see (Press RETURN.) in the exercises, press the return/enter key.

Entering Commands and Text

A word of caution. Sometimes you will need to type letters, words, or phrases in response to questions WordStar will ask you. In the exercise boxes, we have indicated where there should be spaces between words or commands and when you should press the return/enter key. However, sometimes limited space does not allow us to get a complete phrase or command on one line, and sometimes commands that will appear left-justified on your screens are right-justified in the boxes. The important thing is for you not to press the return/enter key unless we specifically tell you to.

You will also enter chunks of text. You should type this information exactly as you see it, pressing the return/enter key at the end of paragraphs and address lines and, when necessary, spacing across the page to the approximate typing position indicated.

And now you are ready to master WordStar!

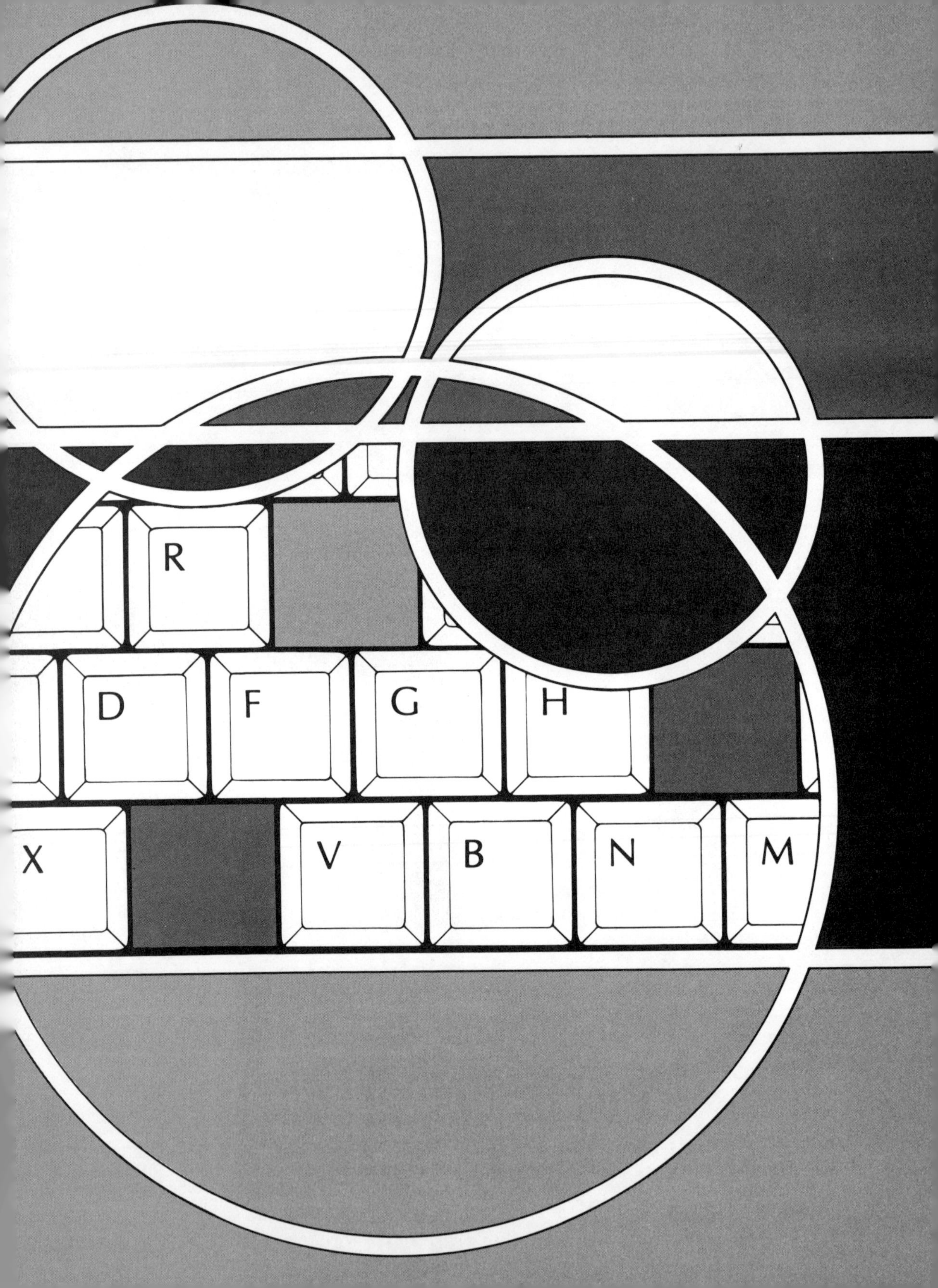
R
D
F
G
H
X
V
B
N
M

PART ONE

An Overview of WordStar

#
3
%
^
6
&
7
*
8
E
Y
S
D
F
H
J
C
V
B
N

one

Getting Past the Disk Operating System

When you purchase a computer with a disk-drive system, you should receive one program disk. This disk contains instructions that tell your computer how to communicate with you, with other parts of the system (such as a printer), and with programs (such as WordStar). This set of instructions is called a disk operating system (DOS). A reputable dealer will make sure that when you buy WordStar you understand how to use DOS and how to make copies of the master (original) program disk.

This chapter provides information about DOS that you as a user of WordStar must understand in order to become an effective word-processing operator. We will define a disk operating system, explain why it is important to a WordStar user, and tell you which one is required by WordStar. Then we will teach you to perform basic CP/M DOS operations, such as waking up your computer, moving around the disk system, and assigning CP/M file names. Finally, we will provide some guidelines to help you choose between CP/M and WordStar file commands.

WHAT IS A DISK OPERATING SYSTEM?

Imagine that you never learned to drive a car. How can you take advantage of the capabilities of an automobile? Well, you can hire a driver who is familiar with the operation of the car you own and who knows how to get around town. When you want to go somewhere, you just hop in the back seat and instruct your driver to take you where you want to go. You don't have to worry about the mechanics of driving, nor do you need to know the best route to your destination—you let the driver worry about those details.

That is the service that a disk operating system provides—it acts as the driver of your computer. It understands the operation of the computer, knows how to get around the various parts of the system, and also communicates with whoever is sitting in the back seat (you, the user, and a program like WordStar).

Which DOS Is Required by WordStar?

Like many back-seat drivers, WordStar is particular about the disk operating systems it is willing to talk to. It will only talk to an operating system called CP/M (Control Program for Microcomputers), to one of CP/M's derivative versions such as MP/M, or to IBM PC-DOS. You should have purchased WordStar only if your computer system uses one of these operating systems.

A word of caution: IBM PC-DOS Version 2.0 requires more of your computer's internal memory (RAM) to operate than its predecessor, Version 1.1. If you have Version 2.0, you will need at least 96K bytes of memory, and preferably 128K bytes, to operate WordStar.

What Is So Important about DOS?

When you turn on your computer, the only thing it knows how to do is check the disk drive hoping to find a disk with DOS stored on it, so that DOS can tell it what to do. A disk that contains the disk operating system is sometimes called a system disk. If the computer does not find a system disk in the drive, it will become confused. Because its only built-in instruction is to find the operating system, it will continue to check the drive until the drive wears out, you turn the poor thing off, or you finally insert a system disk to give the computer some direction in life.

Since DOS tells your computer where to go and how to get there, you can control the whole computer system if you know how to control DOS. Conversely, without DOS you will not be able to go anywhere. DOS manages your disk filing system for you, storing, retrieving, and tracking all the files stored on the disk. A program like WordStar will only operate in conjunction with DOS.

The WordStar program disk you purchased does not have a copy of DOS stored on it. This is because MicroPro did not write and does not sell any DOS—their WordStar program just takes advantage of the maintenance skills of DOS produced by other companies. So one of your first tasks is to copy the WordStar program onto a disk that already has CP/M or IBM PC-DOS stored on it.[1]

Once you have copied WordStar, it becomes a program file stored on your system disk. When you want to use it you will have to ask your file clerk (DOS) to retrieve the WordStar file for you. However, WordStar only likes doing one thing—processing words. When it comes time to perform dull chores like storing information on the disk, or finding, reading, or erasing files, it passes the job back to the program specifically designed to perform those operational functions—you guessed it—DOS. So you can see that it is important that you understand some of the basic operations of your DOS, whether it is CP/M or PC-DOS.

HOW TO PERFORM BASIC CP/M OPERATIONS

There are a few basic CP/M operations that are appropriate for discussion here because they are very important to you, the WordStar user. The time you spend learning the basics of CP/M will make it much easier for you to learn WordStar, because WordStar uses many CP/M conventions. We have used CP/M version 2.1 in our examples.

For a review of additional CP/M operations, read Appendix B: *More Help with CP/M*. If you need help with IBM PC-DOS, read Appendix C: *Basic IBM PC-DOS Operations*.

Waking Up Your Computer

Waking up your computer means turning it on, inserting a system disk in a disk drive, and preparing the computer to start accepting commands from you. This is known as booting the system.

Regardless of how many disk drives are attached to the system, your computer will always check the same drive each time it is turned on. This drive, generally marked *drive A* or *drive 1*, is the one into

[1] This is not the appropriate place to go into great detail about putting CP/M on a disk, because this operation is a little different with each brand of microcomputer. Please check with your computer dealer or read your CP/M manuals or a good reference book like *The CP/M Handbook*, written by Rodnay Zaks and published by Sybex, to learn how you can create a system disk onto which you can copy WordStar.

which you must insert the system disk (the one that has CP/M on it). CP/M always calls this drive *A,* no matter how yours might actually be marked.

Some computers automatically access drive A when the computer is turned on, so all you have to do is turn on the system and insert the appropriate disk. Other systems wait to access the disk drive until you press a special key to notify the computer that you have inserted a disk holding CP/M. You should know the proper procedure for your own system.

When you have successfully awakened your computer, you will see *A>* on your video screen. This is CP/M's way of saying *Hello, you are using disk drive A. What do you want to do?* This announcement is known as the A prompt, because you are being prompted by your computer to give a command.

Moving around the Disk Operating System

As we have said, your computer always accesses drive A first. If you have two disk drives, you might want to insert a disk into each drive, so that you can access more than one disk of information while you are working. For example, it is sometimes helpful to use a disk that contains only the operating system and the WordStar programs in drive A. You can then insert a data disk in drive B to store the documents you create with WordStar. Because data disks are not cluttered up with the CP/M or WordStar programs, you will be able to store many more pages of text on each data disk. This is also a useful practice if you share your computer with others. You can all use the same CP/M-WordStar disk, but each keep your own data disks, which you insert in drive B whenever you want to work on a document.

Choosing the Right Drive If you insert disks in both drives A and B, you probably will want to be able to look directly at the information you have stored on the disk inserted in drive B. To do this, you must log on to that drive. Logging on means telling the operating system to direct its attention to a specific disk drive. As you know, CP/M automatically logs on to drive A when you first turn on your computer. You can then log on to another drive with the appropriate CP/M command.

Access the information stored on the disk in drive B by typing *B:* and pressing RETURN. Notice that the CP/M prompt now displays *B>* to indicate that you have successfully logged on to drive B. Any commands you give CP/M while B> is displayed will be executed on files stored on the disk inserted in drive B.

Any time you want to switch between disk drives, enter the drive letter you want and a colon and then press RETURN. The appropriately lettered prompt will be displayed on your video screen, and you will be able to execute commands on files stored on the disk in the indicated drive.

If you use this command to switch to drive B when there is no disk inserted in that drive, CP/M will respond with the comment *Bdos Err on B: Bad Sector.* In other words, because CP/M cannot read anything on that drive, it assumes that there is something wrong with the disk. If this happens, you will have to restart your computer by turning it off, then booting a system disk in drive A.

Changing Disks What if you discover that you are working with the wrong disk? What if you use all the available space on a disk? Well, you can remove the disk, turn off the computer, and start over—but there is an easier way.

After removing a disk from any drive and inserting a new one, hold down the control key (^), simultaneously press the letter C, and press RETURN. This CP/M command acts as a reset switch. It clears out anything stored in the internal working memory of your computer (RAM) and takes a fresh look at the disks. When the prompt reappears, you know that CP/M is starting from scratch, as if you had just turned on your computer for the first time.

It is very important that you use the ^C command immediately after you change disks. When you boot the system, CP/M checks the disks inserted in each drive to find out how much information is stored on each one. It holds this information in RAM so it can refer to it before it writes any more information on the disks. When you use the ^C command, CP/M rechecks each disk and updates the storage information it currently holds. If you do not use the ^C command after switching a disk in either drive, CP/M will not know that the storage information it has is incorrect. It will find that out when you ask it to store more information on one of the disks. When CP/M discovers that the information it has does not match the actual storage capacity of either disk, it will refuse to write information on the new disk.

So make it a habit: With CP/M, *always* enter the ^C command after changing disks.

Assigning CP/M File Names

The first thing you do when you set up a manual filing system is assign names to each of the files you want to store. To make sure your file clerk can quickly store and retrieve the files, you must be very careful to assign names that follow a standard format.

Every document you create with WordStar is also a file. CP/M, your computer's file clerk, requires that you assign a name to each computerized file you create. To make sure CP/M can quickly locate any files you have stored on disk, a few important rules have been established for developing file names. You must abide by these conventions. If you don't, CP/M will be unable to use your file names to store information on your disks.

The rules for creating CP/M (and WordStar) file names are:

1. All CP/M file names consist of a maximum of eight contiguous characters. If you try to use more than eight, CP/M will ignore anything past the eighth one. You may use less than eight characters.
2. These characters may be letters (upper- or lowercase), numbers, or some punctation marks. You cannot use the asterisk (*) as part of a file name because CP/M uses this symbol as a special code, nor can you use any of the following: <> . , : ; ? = [ ] .
3. Do not include any spaces between characters.

Following are some examples of acceptable and unacceptable CP/M file names:

Acceptable file names	*Unacceptable file names*	
Testfile	Test File	(no spaces allowed)
June-3	June 3	(no spaces allowed)
NewFiles	New-Files	(too many characters)
5/03-LTR	W*-FILE	(no * allowed; see page 12)

As you have probably realized, there are only so many creative ways to use eight characters in a file name and still have a reasonable chance of guessing what is in the file. To give you more flexibility, CP/M and WordStar allow you to add a file type at the end of the eight-character file name so you can key different types of files. Naturally, there are rules for the development of these file types, too.

1. You may add a period and a maximum of three additional characters to a file name to code different types of files. For example, you might use the file type .MSS to define manuscripts, .LTR to define letters, and .FRM to define forms.
2. Do not use the file type .COM. This is reserved by CP/M to indicate that a file is a command file, a program (list of instructions) that tells the computer how to perform specific functions or applications. For example, the WordStar program is

usually coded WS.COM to let CP/M know that it is a program, not a document file.

3. Do not use the file type .BAK, either. WordStar uses this file type to code backup versions of files that it automatically creates every time you reedit a file. Other file types you cannot use are .OVR, .ASM, and .PRN.

4. Do not include any spaces within the file type or between the file name and the file type. You may use any upper- or lowercase letters, numbers, or any character except the asterisk in the file type.

Following are some examples of acceptable and unacceptable file types:

Acceptable file types	*Unacceptable file types*	
File.305	Test .305	(no spaces allowed)
Sample.Ltr	SampleL.T R	(no spaces allowed)
Read.ME	ReadME.*	(no * allowed; see page 12)

File types reserved for CP/M and WordStar	
PIP.COM	(program file)
INSTALL.COM	(program file)
FILENAME.BAK	(WordStar backup file)

Don't Be Too Clever with File Names! One final comment about file names—for your own sake, be consistent when assigning them!

First of all, you must follow the CP/M rules for file-name assignment or CP/M will refuse to file your documents. Second, if you are too imaginative when you make up file names, you will often find yourself stumped by the meaning of names like M3-56S or LTR35.J/T, even though they had some deep meaning for you when you made them up. If more than one person will be using your system, it is especially important that you all use a standard system for assigning file names. It is amazing how quickly the significance of those clever file names can fade into obscurity!

Finally, it is a good idea to establish and use standard file-type designators so you can use CP/M's convenient wild-card symbol to manage several files at one time.

Using CP/M's Wild-Card Symbol

If you develop and consistently use standard file names, you can instruct CP/M to perform many file-handling operations on whole groups of specified file types. This is where the wild-card symbol, the asterisk, flexes its muscles. After you have typed a CP/M command, you may use the * within a file name to indicate that you wish to perform that function on all files having certain characteristics.

For example, you may want a directory of only your program files. You would type the CP/M directory command followed by *.COM. CP/M would display only those file names ending in .COM, such as WS.COM, PIP.COM, and STAT.COM. Or maybe you want a directory of the letters stored on your disk. You would enter the CP/M directory command followed by LTR*.* to indicate that you only want to view files beginning with the characters LTR. CP/M would display LTRJONES, LTR-6/03.BAK and LTR-6/03. It would not display NEWLTR.603 or SMITH.LTR, however, because these file names do not begin with the specified letters LTR.

You can use the wild-card symbol in conjunction with most CP/M commands to save time managing your disk file system.

HOW TO CHOOSE BETWEEN CP/M AND WORDSTAR FILE COMMANDS

Once you enter WordStar, you will find that you can log on to a different disk drive or perform other file-handling commands using WordStar commands as well as CP/M commands. Which do you choose?

There are some advantages to using CP/M commands to perform file operations. CP/M commands allow you to use the wild-card character, *, to perform the same function on several files with one command. For example, use the CP/M versions of erase and copy commands when you want to erase or copy more than one file at a time.

On the other hand, there are also advantages to using WordStar commands to perform the same functions. Although WordStar does not understand the wild-card concept, it is a much more helpful program than CP/M. When you use the WordStar versions of the erase and copy commands, WordStar prompts you for the information you should supply. So use the WordStar versions of file-handling commands if you can't quite remember the proper sequence for the CP/M versions, or if you just feel more comfortable being asked for the information you should provide.

WHAT YOU SHOULD KNOW BY NOW

- Every computer with a disk drive requires a set of programs or instructions called the disk operating system (DOS).
- DOS is the driver of a computer system. It manages communication between the computer itself and the rest of the system, including you, the user, as well as application programs like WordStar.
- WordStar will only operate on systems using CP/M, one of its derivatives, or IBM PC-DOS.

To communicate comfortably with CP/M, you should be able to perform the following tasks:

- Boot the system, log onto a second disk drive, and know how to reset the computer after changing disks.
- Create file names that match the structure required by CP/M, and use the CP/M wild-card symbol to manage more than one file at a time.
- Know when to use CP/M versions of file commands and when to use WordStar versions of the same commands.

#
3
%
^
6
&
7
*
8
E
Y
S
D
F
H
J
C
V
B
N

two

How WordStar Works

This section explains the different programs that make up WordStar and what you need to do to get going. It also reviews the file-handling characteristics you need to understand in order to use WordStar effectively.

It is important that you understand how WordStar is put together and why it does what it does when you push certain buttons. Once you have a feel for the mechanics of the program, you will be able to develop your own way of preparing documents that best takes advantage of WordStar's capabilities.

HOW TO GET STARTED WITH WORDSTAR

When you purchased WordStar, your computer dealer should have supplied you with one or two WordStar program disks with official MicroPro labels. These are known as master (original) disks, because they have not been used or modified since they were shipped from MicroPro. Either you or your dealer will have to modify the WordStar program before you can use it.

WordStar can be used on many different computers, each with its own type of video screen and printer. Some video screens have special features such as text highlighting or dual intensity, which WordStar can use to make it easier for you to find special sections of text in a document. Some printers are able to create fancy printing formats, such as boldface printing or proportional spacing. WordStar can take advantage of these special features to produce snazzy-looking documents.

However, WordStar needs to be told that your equipment has these special features. MicroPro provides two programs on the master disk that are used to create a customized version of WordStar on your computer system. The two programs are called WSU.COM and INSTALL.COM.

WSU.COM is the uncustomized version of the WordStar program. You cannot run the WSU.COM program because it does not know what kind of computer system you have. Think of the WSU.COM file as a blank contract. You can make it a personal contract by filling in the blanks with information about the equipment you are using.

You or your dealer use INSTALL.COM to fill in the blanks. When you run the INSTALL.COM program, it asks you to indicate the type of video screen and printer you have. As you provide this information, INSTALL.COM fills in the blanks in the WSU.COM program, creating a customized, or installed, copy of WordStar that you will be able to run on your system.

When you use INSTALL.COM to customize WSU.COM, WordStar will ask you what you want to name the installed version of the program. Most people call it WS.COM to differentiate it from WSU.COM. You can call your version of WordStar anything you like, but choose a file name that is easy to remember and use. Throughout this book, we will assume that you have named your working version of the WordStar program WS.COM.

Which WordStar Files Do You Really Need?

If your computer dealer provided you with an installed copy of the WordStar program, you should find several files on the disk when you check the directory, including WS.COM, WSMSGS.OVR, and WSOVLY1.OVR.

These three files must be stored on the disk you insert in drive A to boot the system, or you will be unable to use the WordStar program. If your dealer did not install WordStar for you, you will find WSU.COM, INSTALL.COM, WSMSGS.OVR and WSOVLY1.OVR on your master disk. You must create the WS.COM file by using INSTALL.COM to customize WSU.COM.

WSMSGS.OVR and WSOVLY1.OVR are overlay files. They are parts of the WordStar program that hold additional information the program may need to perform certain functions or to help you use WordStar.

The WSMSGS.OVR file holds all the helpful messages and information that can be displayed on the video screen while you are using WordStar. MicroPro decided not to include these messages in the main WordStar program module, because they would take up too much of your computer's internal memory (RAM), leaving too little room for the document you are writing. Instead, whenever WordStar needs to display a new message or comment, it pulls it out of the WSMSGS.OVR file and puts it in RAM, so that it can be displayed on your video screen. This is a much more efficient use of space than keeping all possible messages in RAM just so one or two of them can be displayed occasionally.

The WSOVLY1.OVR provides miscellaneous program capabilities to support the operation of the main WordStar program. WS.COM and WSOVLY1.OVR have to match. If you somehow manage to mix up old and new versions of WordStar on the same disk so that WS.COM cannot match up with the right WSOVLY1.OVR file, you will be unable to use WordStar. So if you do get an updated version of WordStar that includes new overlay files, be sure to keep your old and new disks separate. Better yet, erase all your old versions. All the documents you created with an old version of WordStar can be accessed by a new version, so why make life more complicated than it needs to be?

What Are All Those Other Files?

When you check the directory of your original WordStar disk, you will also find files whose names end in .TXT or .LTR. These are the sample text and letter files that MicroPro expects you to use to practice the exercises included in the WordStar training manual. Once you have finished practicing, you can erase these files.

Creating a Working WordStar Disk

Once you have installed WordStar, you can make a working WordStar disk by copying WS.COM, WSMSGS.OVR, and WSOVLY1.OVR onto a disk that also contains CP/M or IBM PC-DOS. Use the CP/M or IBM PC-DOS copy programs to copy the files. You do not need to copy WSU.COM or INSTALL.COM because you will never use them again, unless you buy a new terminal or printer that WordStar needs to know about.

You should probably also copy the CP/M or IBM PC-DOS file-copy and disk-capacity status programs onto your working program disk (see Figure 2.1). That way you will be able to use those programs on your WordStar files without having to change disks.

Store your master WordStar disk in a safe place. If you ever damage your working program disk, you can make a new copy from the master.

Now that you have a basic understanding of the components of the

WordStar word-processing system, we will take a look at WordStar's file-handling techniques.

HOW WORDSTAR HANDLES FILES

File handling simply describes a program's way of storing and retrieving information from the internal working memory of a computer (RAM) or a permanent storage medium (such as a floppy disk). Word-processing programs are very dependent on their file-handling capabilities because much of their time is spent moving information

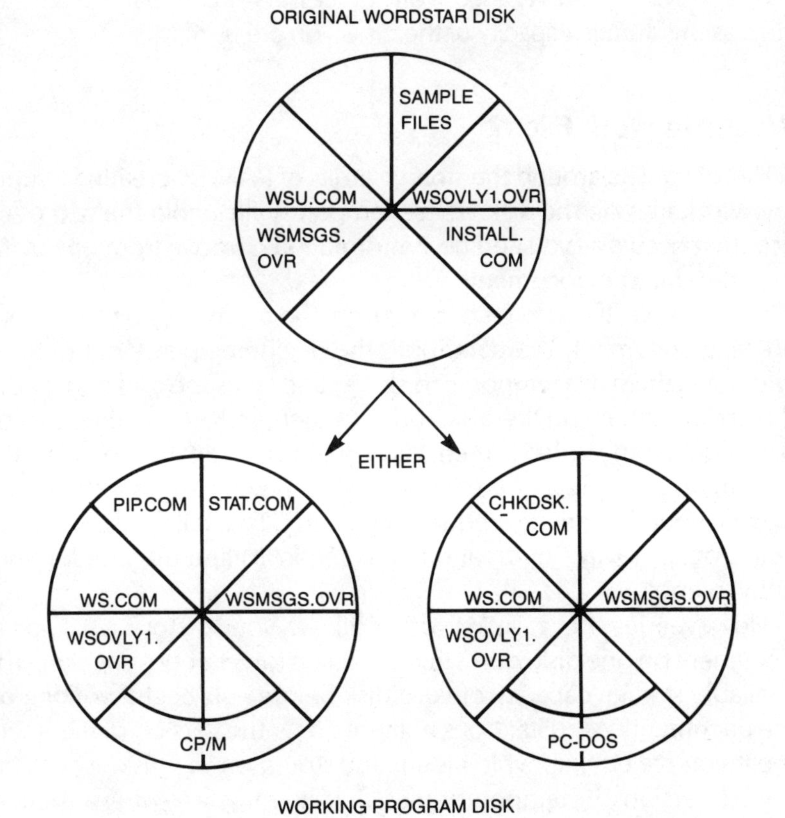

Figure 2.1: *Creating a Working WordStar Disk*

from place to place. It is important for you, the WordStar user, to understand how the program manages files, so that you don't accidentally lose or damage one of your important documents.

As you type a document, it is simultaneously displayed on your computer's video screen and stored in RAM, the computer's internal memory and temporary work space. You might think of your video screen as a window that exposes a small portion of the document stored in RAM.

Some word-processing programs limit the size of each document to the storage capacity of RAM. In most cases, these RAM-based word processors can only accommodate a 15- to 20-page document. WordStar, however, does not limit your documents to the capacity of your computer's RAM. It is a disk-based word processor—it can manage a file as large as the storage capacity of the disks you are using.

What Are Work Files?

WordStar gets around the storage limits of RAM by creating temporary work files on the disk. These temporary files hold the text overflow that occurs as you add new information or move from one place to another in the document.

For example, if you want to jump from the beginning to the end of a 30-page document, WordStar pulls the beginning pages out of RAM and stores them in a temporary disk file, and takes the end pages from the document file on the disk and puts them in RAM so they can be displayed on the video screen. As you jump to different parts of the document entering and editing text, you may notice that the in-use light on your disk drive is frequently glowing. That tells you that WordStar is busy moving information between RAM and the disk for your convenience.

However, just because WordStar allows you to store a 100-page document on one disk, don't think you can forget about checking the available storage capacity of your disk before you begin working on the document! WordStar does not write over the version of the document you are editing, which is already stored on the disk. It puts the edited versions in temporary files that it stores anywhere there is space on the disk. So while you are editing or moving around in your 100-page document, WordStar is creating temporary disk files that can take up an additional 100 pages of space.

Of course, once you finish editing the document and tell WordStar to save it, WordStar will pull all those temporary files together, erase any it does not need, and store the final version on the disk, all in one place (see Figure 2.2).

If you frequently edit large documents, protect yourself by confirming before you begin that at least twice as much disk storage space is available as will be required for the finished document. If you discover that there is not twice as much, there are three operations you

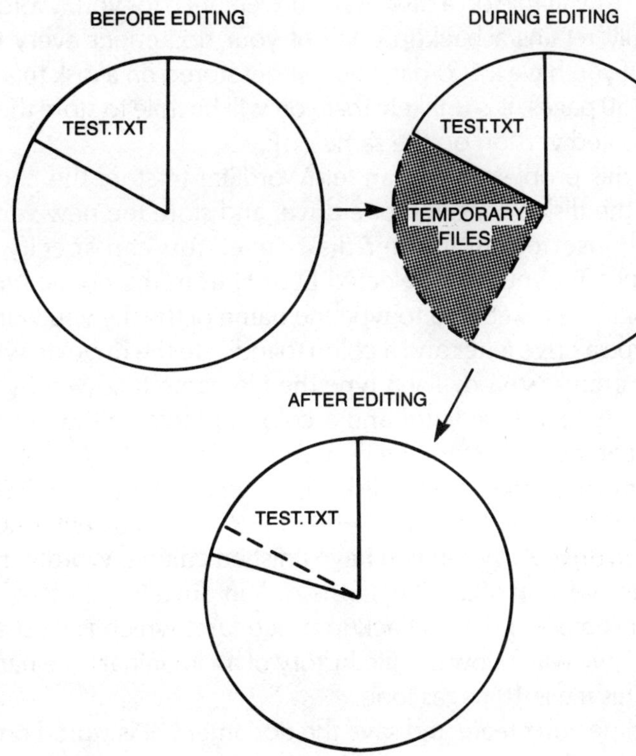

Figure 2.2: *Disk Space Needed By Your Document*

can perform to make enough space:

- Delete files you do not expect to need again.
- Copy files you do want to save onto another disk, then erase the versions stored on the disk you are using now.
- Prepare a fresh disk on which you can store the large document you want to edit.

What Are Backup Files?

There is another reason why you should be constantly aware of the storage space available on a disk. As a convenience for you, WordStar automatically retains a backup copy of your document every time you edit it. If you have a 100-page document stored on a disk that can only store 150 pages, it is unlikely that you will be able to store the old and the updated version on the same disk.

To avoid this problem, you can tell WordStar to store the backup version on the disk inserted in one drive, and store the new version on the disk inserted in another disk drive. You can specify this arrangement after you have selected D or N from the no-file menu, and WordStar has asked you to type the name of the file you want to edit. First type a drive letter and a colon to indicate the drive on which the file is currently stored. Then type the file name followed by one space. Then type a drive letter and a colon to indicate the drive on which WordStar should store the new version of the file. The old version will remain on the original disk. For example, type A:LETTER B: to tell WordStar to edit the file called LETTER that is currently stored on the disk in drive A. When you have finished editing, WordStar will store the new version of the file on the disk in drive B.

To demonstrate WordStar's backup procedure, which is illustrated in Figure 2.3,we will follow the file history of an imaginary file named TEST.TXT. This file is 10 pages long.

The first time you create and save the document, it is stored on the disk using the file name you have given it. After you proofread a printed copy of the original document, you decide you want to edit it. You call for it by name, TEST.TXT. WordStar displays a copy of the file on your video screen so that you can edit it. The original version remains on the disk.

Once you have finished editing the copy of the document, you tell WordStar to store the edited version on the disk. Knowing that this is the most current version of your document, WordStar names this edited version TEST.TXT. The original version remains on the disk, but now it is called TEST.BAK. Its file name tells you it is the old version of the document. If you check the disk directory after storing the edited version, you will see a file named TEST.TXT and a file named TEST.BAK. Because you have two copies of the 10-page file stored on disk, you now have used 20 pages of disk space.

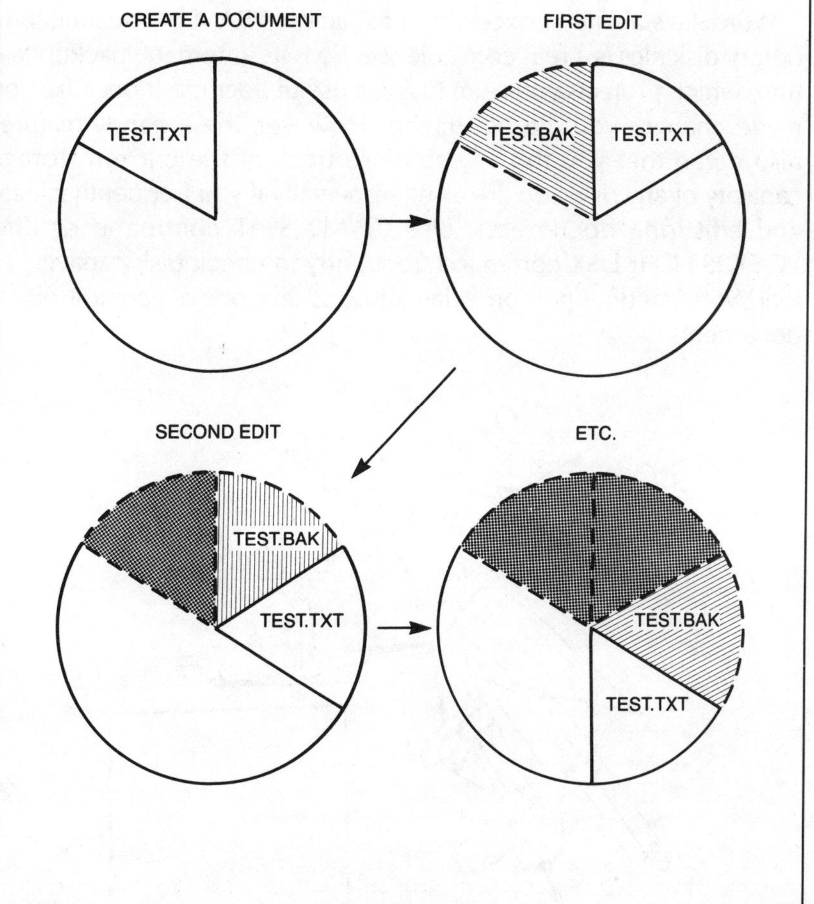

Figure 2.3: *WordStar's Backup Procedure*

What happens if you edit TEST.TXT again? First, you call for it using the file name TEST.TXT. WordStar displays a copy of the most recent version of the document. After you edit it, you again instruct WordStar to save the file. Because this third version is now the most current version, WordStar labels it TEST.TXT. It then renames the second version TEST.BAK and erases the original version of the document. So again, your 10-page document requires 20 pages of disk storage.

From now on, whenever you edit and save TEST.TXT, WordStar names the new version TEST.TXT, renames the previous version TEST.BAK, and erases the version created two generations ago. Getting confused? Study Figure 2.3 to get a better idea of how WordStar makes backup files.

WordStar's ability to exceed the capacity of RAM by creating temporary disk files is a real convenience. So is its automatic backup feature, which protects you from losing a useful document because you made changes you did not intend. However, these handy features also mean that you must keep close track of the current storage capacity of any disk you are using, especially if you frequently create and edit long documents. Use CP/M's STAT command or IBM PC-DOS's CHKDSK command frequently to check disk capacity, so that WordStar does not some day refuse to save one of your important documents.

WHAT YOU SHOULD KNOW BY NOW

- You use the WordStar files named WSU.COM and INSTALL.COM once to create a version of WordStar tailored to your system's video screen and printer. Then you should store the WordStar master disk containing them in a safe place, because you will not need to use it again unless you change systems.
- In order for you to use WordStar, your working program disk must include a copy of the disk operating system (CP/M or IBM PC-DOS), the customized version of the WSU.COM program (probably named WS.COM), and the overlay files WSMSGS.OVR and WSOVLY1.OVR.
- WordStar is a disk-based word processor, meaning that it creates temporary work files on the disk while you are editing a document. In this way, it makes more space available in the temporary memory of the computer (RAM) so that you can create larger documents. It is a good idea to make sure before you begin editing that the disk has twice as much storage space available as the estimated finished size of the document.
- When you store an edited version of a document, WordStar automatically preserves the previous version and renames it by changing its file type to .BAK.

#
3
%
^
6
&
7
*
8
E
Y
S
D
F
H
J
C
V
B
N

three

A Walk through the WordStar Maze

As you worked your way through WordStar's training manual, you were introduced to its different modules. Each WordStar module is a part of the WordStar program that has its own menu or video display of the functions you can perform when you are in that module.

Think of the WordStar program as a maze. It may seem a bit bewildering at first. How are you ever going to find your way around those modules well enough to be able to use them efficiently? But don't worry; you will soon be able to go smoothly from one to another without getting lost!

To get into the WordStar maze, you must enter an anteroom, where you will find a series of doors leading off in different directions. Each one of these doors is the entrance to a different part of the maze. Once inside the maze, you can sometimes pass directly from one section to another; sometimes you must return to the anteroom and explore a new section from there.

This section provides an overview of WordStar's anteroom and the different parts of the WordStar maze. It does not provide the detailed information available in the WordStar training manual or *Introduction to WordStar* by Arthur Naiman. It is intended to refresh your memory of what you learned in those two introductory guides.

HOW TO ENTER THE MAZE: THE NO-FILE MENU

To enter the anteroom of WordStar's maze, type the name of the customized version of the WordStar program file stored on your disk. Do not type the file type code .COM that is appended to the name. In most cases, you will type WS and press RETURN.

On your video screen you will see a display of the commands you can use to enter other parts of the program (see Figure 3.1). This display, called the no-file menu, will only appear on your screen when you are not creating or editing a document. The no-file menu commands are categorized by function.

Getting Started

Preliminary commands control the computer's operating environment. They duplicate similar CP/M and IBM PC-DOS commands. They are called preliminary commands because you normally set the operating functions listed in this section before you begin writing or editing a document. For example, you can use a no-file menu command to log on to another disk drive, just as you would use the drive number or letter followed by a colon if you were in CP/M. You can also use a preliminary command to display or omit the directory of files

```
editing no file
              < < <      N O   F I L E    M E N U        > > >

- - -Preliminary Commands- - -   | - -File Commands- - | -System Commands-
L  Change logged disk drive      |                     | R  Run a program
F  File directory off (ON)       | P  Print a file     | X  EXIT to system
H  Set help level                |                     |
 - - -Commands to Open a file- - -| E  RENAME a file   | -WordStar Options-
D  Open a document file          | O  COPY a file      | M  Run MailMerge
N  Open a non-document file      | Y  DELETE a file    | S  Run SpellStar   ▲

DIRECTORY of disk A:
 MAILMRGE.OVR    WS.COM    WSMSGS.OVR    WSOVLY1.OVR
```

Figure 3.1: *The No-File Menu*

stored on the logged disk, just as you would use the DIR command in CP/M. The final preliminary command adjusts the amount of helpful information you want WordStar to display as you use the program.

Opening a File

Commands to open a file are used to tell WordStar the name of the document you want to write or to enter the name of an existing document you want to edit. Once you enter a file name, you will be transferred to WordStar's edit mode to begin work on the document.

Manipulating Files

File commands are used to manipulate whole documents (files) once they have been created. Most of these commands operate similarly to their relatives in CP/M. They are included in the no-file menu as a convenience, so that you do not have to exit to CP/M every time you want to rename, copy, or delete a file.

Remember, when you need to use the CP/M wild-card character * to handle more than one file at a time, use the CP/M versions of these file commands. Sometimes the WordStar versions are more convenient. WordStar asks you for the information you must provide, so you can also use the WordStar commands when you cannot remember what information to enter.

Moving between WordStar and DOS

System commands allow you to leave WordStar to return to CP/M or IBM PC-DOS (the system). They also allow you to run DOS programs without actually leaving WordStar. The most common reason for using a system command is to run the CP/M program STAT or the IBM PC-DOS program CHKDSK to find out how much space is left on a disk.

Using WordStar with Other Programs

WordStar options are used to run two programs that MicroPro has developed to enhance the WordStar program. The command M runs

MailMerge, MicroPro's mailing-list program. The command S runs SpellStar, their spelling-checker program. Both programs can only be used if you have stored them on your WordStar program disk.

When you select any one of these entry-level commands, you open a door from the anteroom into a different section of the WordStar maze. There are six sections in all. Once you enter one of these sections or modules, you are presented with a new menu of options, each of which will lead you further into the WordStar program.

For an overview of the maze, take a few minutes to study Figure 3.2. Notice that some sections lead directly to other parts of the program, avoiding return to the no-file menu.

THE EDIT-MODE MAIN MENU

When you first enter WordStar's edit mode, its main menu will be displayed on your screen (see Figure 3.3). This menu includes most of the commands you will use regularly to create and edit documents. Like the no-file menu, the commands listed in the edit-mode main menu are categorized by function.

Moving the Cursor

Cursor-movement commands are used to reposition the cursor anywhere within the text displayed on the video screen. The cursor tells you which character or space on the screen the computer is looking at. You will learn these cursor commands quickly because you have to move the cursor to the location of an error before you can delete or correct it.

Scrolling commands are used to display different sections of a document on the video screen. They enable you to move from one page to another so that you can enter text or make corrections.

Editing Documents

Delete commands are used to erase incorrect characters, words, or lines of text. These commands permanently remove information from a document.

Miscellaneous commands include most of the other commonly

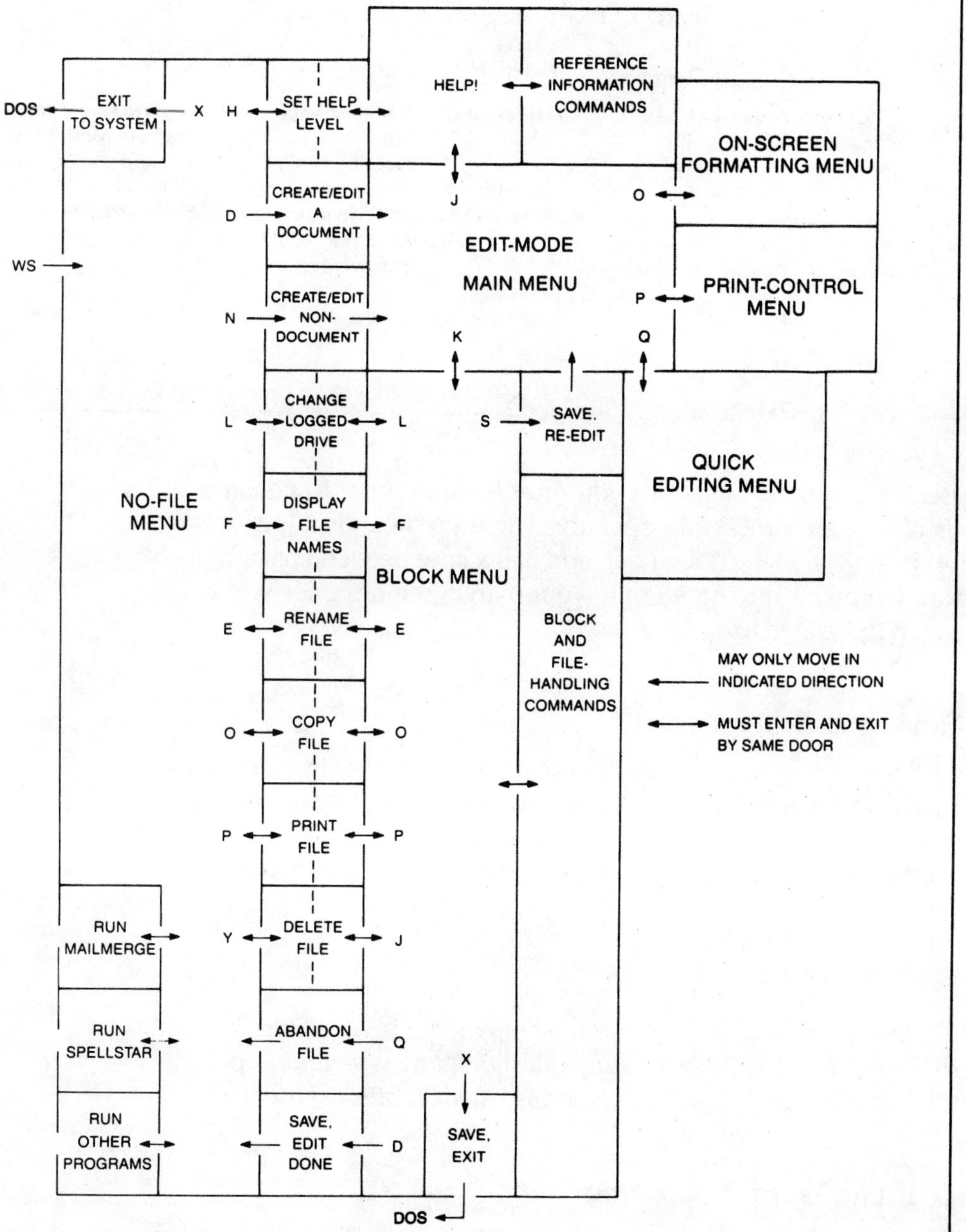

Figure 3.2: *The WordStar Maze*

```
     A:PRACTICE.DOC    PAGE 1  LINE 1  COL 01              INSERT ON

                      <<<      M A I N  M E N U        >>>

     - -Cursor Movement- -     |  -Delete-  |   -Miscellaneous-     |   -Other  Menus-
^S char left   ^D char right   | ^G  char   | ^I  Tab    ^B Reform  |   (from Main only)
^A word left   ^F word right   | DEL chr lf | ^V  INSERT ON/OFF     | ^J Help    ^K Block
^E line up     ^X line down    | ^T  word rt| ^L  Find/Replce again | ^Q Quick   ^P Print
       - -Scrolling- -         | ^Y  line   | RETURN End paragraph  | ^O Onscreen
^Z line up     ^W line down    |            | ^N  Insert a RETURN   |
^C screen up   ^R screen down  |            | ^U  Stop a command    |

L- - - -!- - - -!- - - -!- - - -!- - - -!- - - -!- - - -!- - - -!- - - -!- - - -!- - - - - - - - -R
▲
```

Figure 3.3: *The Edit-Mode Main Menu*

used editing commands that you must learn in order to become an effective word-processing operator. These commands allow you to insert text within the document, add blank lines between paragraphs, and reformat text to conform to your margin settings once you have added or deleted text.

Moving to Other Menus

Other menus commands list the keys you must press in order to display any one of the other edit-mode menus. These menus are sometimes called control-key menus because you have to press ^ (CONTROL or CTRL) as part of each menu-display command.

THE ^J MENU

The ^J menu, also known as the help menu, is WordStar's answer to the common word-processing question *Now where did I put the reference manual?* WordStar's response: *Look in the ^J menu.*

Learning Word Processing

When you select the appropriate key, WordStar will teach you how to reform a paragraph, how to format and use dot commands, how to

```
^J  A:PRACTICE.DOC  PAGE 1   LINE 1   COL 01              INSERT ON
                 <<<        H E L P   M E N U        >>>
                                        |                     |  - -Other Menus- -
H Display & set the help level          | S  Status line      |   (from Main only)
B Paragraph reform (CONTROL-B)          | R  Ruler line       |  ^J  Help      ^K Block
F Flags in right-most column            | M  Margins & Tabs   |  ^Q  Quick     ^P Print
D Dot commands, print controls          | P  Place markers    |  ^O  Onscreen
                                        | V  Moving text      |  Space bar returns
                                                              |  you to Main Menu.
L- - - -!- - - -!- - - -!- - - -!- - - -!- - - -!- - - -!- - - -!- - - -!- - - - - - R
```

Figure 3.4: *The ^J Menu*

set and use margins, tabs, and place markers, and how to move sections of text. It will also suggest simple ways to prepare special document layouts. Once you make a selection, WordStar takes over your video screen and displays everything it knows about your chosen topic. If the information requires more than one screen display, you can press the space bar to display the next page.

Perhaps you have forgotten what some of WordStar's code symbols mean? When you select the correct command key, WordStar will explain the significance of some of the special symbols and codes it displays on your video screen, such as the flags displayed to the right of each line of text.

Setting the Help Level

WordStar includes all sorts of helpful prompts and menus of information that appear throughout the program. It will give you as much or as little help as you need. When you are just learning to use WordStar, it is great to have the menus displayed on your video screen to remind you of commands and operating procedures. However, once you become comfortable with the program, it can be irritating to wade through prompts you do not need. You can select a command from the ^J menu to adjust the amount of helpful information WordStar displays on the screen while you are working.

THE ^K MENU

The ^K menu lists commands that allow you to manipulate blocks of text. A block may be either a whole document or sections of text within one document. You may use ^K commands to move, copy, delete, and store (or save) sections of text and to move, copy, delete, save, and print whole documents.

Saving Documents

You can use ^K commands to save a document on a disk and then go back to the no-file menu or directly to DOS. There is also a ^K command that updates the version of the document stored on a disk while you are editing it, so that you are protected against losing all the work you have in RAM if there is a power failure. If you decide you do not want to keep the document you are editing, you can use a ^K command to abandon the document without saving it.

Setting Markers

By setting temporary place markers with a ^K command, you can quickly skip to different marked sections of a document.

```
^K   A:PRACTICE.DOC   PAGE 1   LINE 1   COL 01              INSERT ON
                  < < <        B L O C K   M E N U        > > >
-Saving Files-     | -Block Operations-   | -File Operations-       |   -Other Menus-
S Save & resume    | B Begin   K  End     | R  Read     P  Print    |  (from Main only)
D Save  done       | H Hide / Display     | O  Copy     E  Rename   | ^J Help    ^K Block
X Save & exit      | C Copy    Y  Delete  | J  Delete               | ^Q Quick   ^P Print
Q Abandon file     | V Move    W  Write   | -Disk Operations-       | ^O Onscreen
-Place Markers-    | N Column on (OFF)    | L Change logged disk    | Space bar returns
0 9 set/hide 0 9   |                      | F Directory on (OFF)    | you to Main Menu.
L- - - -!- - - -!- - - -!- - - -!- - - -!- - - -!- - - -!- - - -!- - - -!- - - -!- - - - - - - -R
```

Figure 3.5: *The ^K Menu*

Manipulating Documents

You can also use ^K commands to perform operations similar to those in the no-file menu. You can copy documents to other disks, print them, rename them, or erase them. You can also change the logged disk drive, and you can turn on and off the video display of the names of files stored on the logged drive.

THE ^Q MENU

Many of the commands found in the ^Q menu are used to speed up functions performed by commands listed in the edit-mode main menu.

Moving the Cursor Quickly

By adding the command ^Q to the beginning of the main-menu cursor-movement and scrolling commands, you can move the cursor more quickly through a document. For example, you may recall that the main-menu command ^S moves the cursor one character to the left. Well, by entering the command ^QS, you can move the cursor all the way to the left margin.

```
^Q     A:PRACTICE.DOC    PAGE 1   LINE 1   COL 01            INSERT ON

                 <<<       Q U I C K   M E N U       >>>

  ---Cursor Movement---   | -Delete-  |  --Miscellaneous--  |   --Other  Menus--
S left side   D right side | Y  line rt| F Find text in file |  (from Main only)
E top scrn    X bottom scrn| DEL lin lf| A Find & Replace    | ^J Help    ^K Block
R top file    C end file              | L Find Misspelling  | ^Q Quick   ^P Print
B top block   K end block             | Q Repeat command or | ^O Onscreen
0-9 marker    Z up     W down         |   key until space   | Space bar returns
P previous    V last Find or Block    |   bar or other key  | you to Main Menu.
L----!----!----!----!----!----!----!----!----!----!----!----------R
```

Figure 3.6: *The ^Q Menu*

Controlling Deletion

By adding the command ^ Q to the beginning of the main-menu command ^ Y which deletes a line, you can delete part of a line.

Finding and Replacing Words

You can use the command ^ QF to find every occurrence of a word in a document. You can use the command ^ QA to find every occurrence of a word, then replace it with another word that you specify.

Repeating Commands

If you enter the command ^ QQ, WordStar automatically repeats the next command you enter. It will continue to repeat the command until you interrupt the process by pressing the space bar. For example, you can reform an entire document by moving the cursor to the beginning of the document and entering the command ^ QQ ^ B. WordStar will automatically move through the entire document, reforming every paragraph it passes.

THE ^ P MENU

The ^ P menu is WordStar's printer-control menu. You use the commands listed in this menu to create special printing characteristics.

Creating Special Effects

You can use ^ P commands to create **boldface** print, which, as you can see, appears darker and fatter on the page. WordStar creates boldface print by telling your printer to type a character, then back up a fraction of a space and retype the same character. Because the second character does not quite line up over the first character, the finished character looks a little fatter as well as darker than a character that is typed only once. If you want to print characters that are darker, but not fatter, you can use a ^ P command to create *double-strike* characters. These are characters that the printer types twice, with the second impression perfectly aligned over the first printing. Other ^ P

```
^P     A:PRACTICE.DOC   PAGE 1   LINE 1   COL 01              INSERT ON
                  < < <        P R I N T   M E N U        > > >
 - - - - - - Special  Effects - - - - - -  |   -Printing Changes-    |  -Other  Menus-
 (begin and end)   |  (one time each)      | A Alternate pitch       |  (from Main only)
B Bold  D Double   | H Overprint char      | N Standard pitch        | ^J Help   ^K Block
 S Underscore      | O Non break space     | C Printing pause        | ^Q Quick  ^P Print
 X Strikeout       | F Phantom space       | Y Other ribbon color    | ^O Onscreen
 V Subscript       | G Phantom rubout      |   - -User  Patches- -   | Space Bar returns
 T Superscript     | RET Overprint line    | Q(1)  W(2)  E(3)  R(4)  | you to Main Menu.
L- - - -!- - - -!- - - -!- - - -!- - - -!- - - -!- - - -!- - - -!- - - -!- - - - - - - - -R
```

Figure 3.7: *The ^ P Menu*

commands will underline or strike over characters or create sub- and superscripts.

Controlling the Printer

Other ^ P commands will alternate between 10-pitch and 12-pitch typefaces, and between the top and bottom colors of a dual-color ribbon. You can also use a ^ P menu command to tell the printer to pause temporarily so that you can change printwheels or ribbons.

THE ^ O MENU

The commands found in the ^ O menu are used to change the on-screen appearance of your document by altering its physical format. In general, WordStar prints a document the way it appears on your screen—what you see is what you get—so it is important that you know how to control the on-screen appearance.

Changing Line Formats

You can use other commands found in the ^ O menu to center lines of text automatically, as well as change spacing between lines (for example, to print double- or triple-space).

Changing Margins and Tabs

Using ^O commands, you can set left and right margins and change the tab settings. You can also temporarily indent the left margin for outline formats, as well as temporarily release the right margin so you can type a line that is longer than the established margin setting.

Overriding Standard Display Features

You can also use ^O commands to turn off some of the automatic display features built into WordStar. These features include wordwrap, which automatically moves words down to the beginning of the next line as you type, and justification, which perfectly aligns each line of text so that it creates an even right-hand margin. You can also eliminate the display of page breaks, the ruler line that indicates current margin and tab settings, and special ^P-command markers, so that you will not be distracted by their appearance on the screen.

DOT COMMANDS

There is one other type of command that you can use to control the finished appearance of your documents. It does not appear on any of WordStar's menus, though it is explained in the helpful ^J menu. This

```
^O   A:PRACTICE.DOC   PAGE 1   LINE 1   COL 01            INSERT ON
              <<<     O N S C R E E N   M E N U      >>>
-Margins & Tabs-   | -Line Functions-     |  - -More Toggles- -      | -Other Menus-
L Set left margin  | C Center text        | J Justify    off (ON)    | (from Main only)
R Set right margin | S Set line spacing   | V Vari-tabs  off (ON)    | ^J Help     ^K Block
X Release margins  |                      | H Hyph-help  off (ON)    | ^Q Quick    ^P Print
I Set   N Clear tab|    - - -Toggles- - - | E Soft hyph  on  (OFF)   | ^O Onscreen
G Paragraph tab    | W Wrd wrap off (ON)  | D Prnt disp  off (ON)    | Space bar returns
F Ruler from line  | T Rlr line off (ON)  | P Pge break  off (ON)    | you to Main Menu.

L- - - -!- - - -!- - - -!- - - -!- - - -!- - - -!- - - -!- - - -!- - - -!- - - - - - - - -R
```

Figure 3.8: *The ^O Menu*

type of command is called a dot command because each command begins with a dot (period).

You use dot commands to override certain standard WordStar printing features, either throughout a whole document or in certain portions of a document. WordStar will only act on dot commands that follow a specified format:

1. All dot commands begin with a period.
2. The period must appear in column 1, regardless of the left margin you have set. Whenever WordStar encounters a period in column 1, it knows that the information that follows will be a command.
3. There may not be any blank spaces between the period and the command letters which follow it. There may be spaces between the command letters and any number which specifies the range of the command.
4. You may not place more than one dot command on a line.
5. You may not type any text you want printed on the same line as a dot command.

If you do not adhere to these rules when entering dot commands, WordStar will ignore the command or print it as text in the body of the document.

Controlling Page Layout

You can use dot commands to set top and bottom margins, offset the left margin from the edge of the paper, and indicate the number of lines that should appear on each page, the number of characters printed per horizontal inch (pitch), and the number of lines printed per vertical inch.

Controlling Special Formats

Other dot commands allow you to control the location of the page number on each page and to insert automatic headlines at the top or footers at the bottom of each page.

WHAT YOU SHOULD KNOW BY NOW

- The no-file menu is the anteroom or entrance to the WordStar maze. When you tell CP/M that you want to use WordStar, the no-file menu appears on your screen to allow you to make a selection and begin using the program.
- The edit-mode main menu appears once you tell WordStar that you want to begin creating or editing a document. This menu lists most of the commands you will use to edit your work.
- Five special menus can be called up by entering the control-key command that names the menu. If you know which special menu command you want to use, you may enter it without waiting for WordStar to display the appropriate menu.
- The ^J menu is WordStar's on-screen reference manual. Use this menu whenever you need to remind yourself how to perform a WordStar function.
- The ^K menu allows you to manipulate blocks of text or whole documents. Use this menu to cut-and-paste text or to save a completed document onto a disk.
- The ^Q menu enhances many of the main-menu commands. Use this menu to move more quickly through a document, delete more text at one time, repeat a command, or find and replace text rapidly.
- The ^P menu produces special printed effects. Use this menu to add a little pizzazz to your documents by highlighting text, underlining it, or creating sub- and superscripts.
- The ^O menu changes the on-screen appearance of your document. Use this menu to change margins and tabs, center text, or turn on and off WordStar formatting features like wordwrap.

- Dot commands are special commands that you enter within a document to change the way it will look when printed. If you follow the rules for dot commands, you will be able to control page layout and page number placement, as well as insert special comments at the top and bottom of each page.

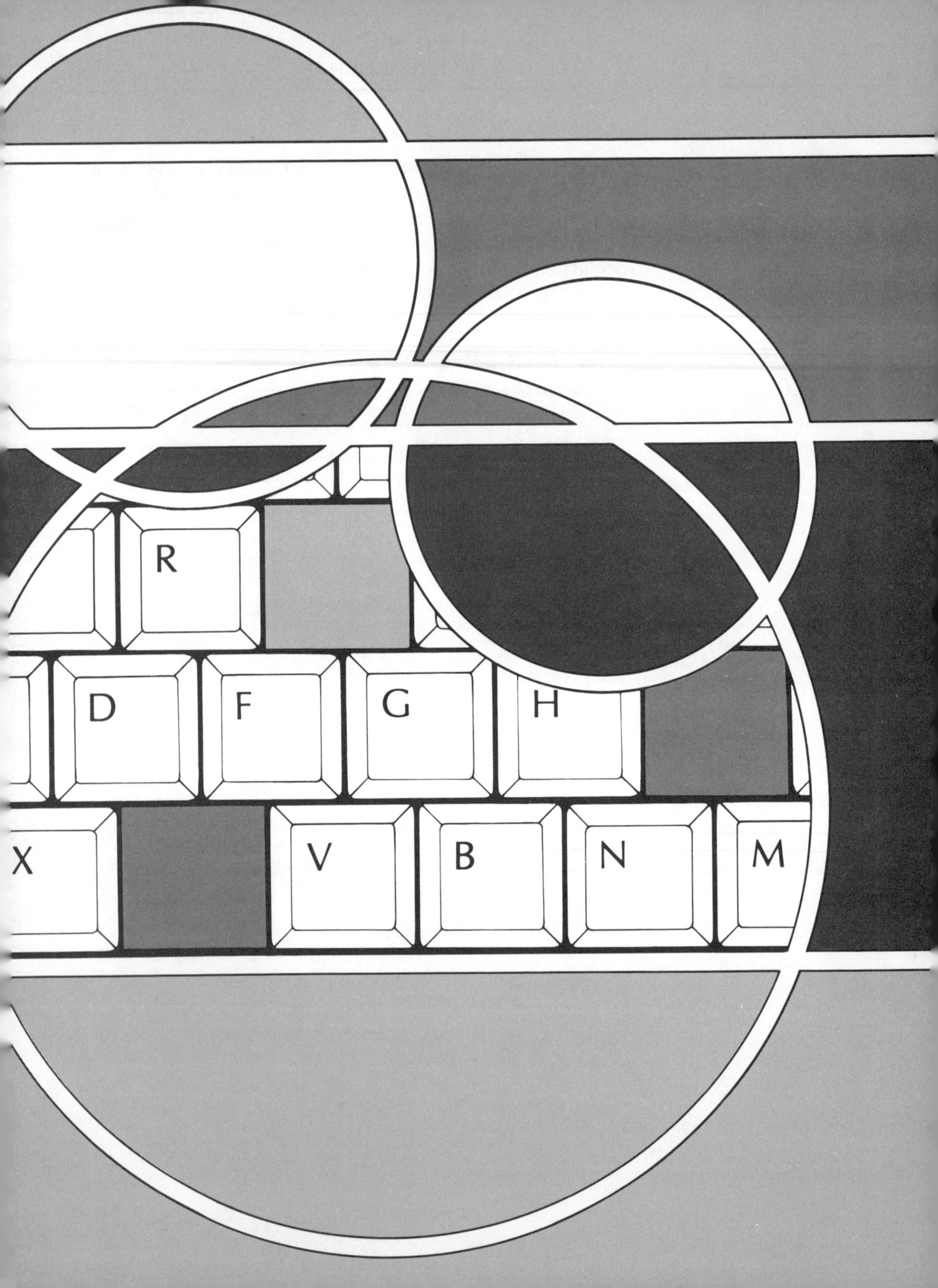
R
D
F
G
H
X
V
B
N
M

PART TWO

WordStar Applications

#
3
%
^
6
&
7
*
8
Y
S
D
F
H
J
C
V
B
N

four
Introduction

Though you may be comfortable using WordStar's most basic commands, you may still find it difficult to put them all together to create the types of documents you need. That is why the rest of this book is a comprehensive, step-by-step introduction to the development of commonly used word-processing formats and techniques. As you work through the following exercises, you will begin to understand the amazing power of WordStar.

The 11 exercises in this section include different WordStar cheater techniques to cut your typing time, and different ways to create special formats for your documents. You can apply any of the cheater techniques to your own documents, and you can modify any of the formats to fit your own needs.

Each exercise begins with a brief discussion of the type of application you will be developing, including some suggestions of similar documents to which you can apply the same techniques. The development process is then briefly outlined so that you understand ahead of time what you are doing as you follow the instructions.

Then you will be led step-by-step through the actual preparation and use of the application. We have invented an imaginary business whose correspondence, announcements, and contracts you will be typing as you hone your word-processing skills. To let you know what to do next, *WordStar Comments and Important Notes* are given in the wide, outer column of each page, and the information you should enter or instructions you should follow are given in the narrow,inner column. First read the numbered comments in the outer column, then enter whatever appears in the inner column.

In our instructions, we assume that you are using two disk drives, one for the WordStar program files and one for your text files. We suggest that you insert your WordStar disk in drive A and load it. Then insert a blank, formatted disk in drive B and log onto that drive. When you are logged on to drive B, your computer knows to go back to drive A for program instructions but to store and retrieve document files on the disk in drive B. This is good standard practice whenever you use WordStar.

Finally, each exercise ends with a summary of the steps you took to complete the application, which you can use later to jog your memory.

WHERE TO BEGIN

The exercises are presented in ascending order of difficulty. If you are a beginner, we encourage you to try each application in sequence because some of the applications build on knowledge you will have gained in previous exercises.

If you are an intermediate or expert WordStar operator, you are welcome to try the exercises in any order you like (if you don't mind missing a day or two in the life of our imaginary company!). However, to cut typing time we have used some documents in more than one application, so you might be forced to work a few exercises just to get the document you need for a later application. Don't think of it as a waste of time—you might learn something new!

WHAT EQUIPMENT AND SKILLS DO YOU NEED?

To use this workbook, you must have an operational computer system, including a printer. You must also have a version of WordStar that will work on your system.

Your skills must include the ability to boot the system and move from CP/M to WordStar's no-file menu. You should also be comfortable entering and editing text so that you can correct any typographical errors you may make. We will tell you anything else you need to know to prepare these applications as we go along.

Oh yes, one more instruction. Have fun!

#
3
%
^
6
&
7
*
8
E
Y
S
D
F
H
J
C
V
B
N

five
Mini-Glossaries

WHAT IS A MINI-GLOSSARY?

Some word processors include a phrase glossary, in which you can store often-used words or phrases. As you are typing, you can enter a special code that will tell the program to insert a glossary word or phrase automatically at that location. This feature eliminates repetitive typing of company names, titles, or phrases.

WordStar does not really have a built-in glossary, but we have developed a technique that allows you to use some of WordStar's commands to create a mini-glossary for individual documents.

WHEN TO USE A MINI-GLOSSARY

If you are typing a document that includes many references to your name, your company name, or a certain product, use this technique to save yourself the trouble of repetitively typing the same information. For example, we used this technique when preparing the manuscript for this book, so we did not have to type the word *WordStar* every time we wanted to refer to the program. You might also use this technique to insert a standard comment or phrase (such as *Press RETURN*) automatically in many different parts of a document.

Use this technique when you have only one repeated word or phrase that you want to insert. You cannot use this technique if the document you are typing includes two or more repetitive phrases, because WordStar can only remember one word or phrase at a time. In the next exercise, we will show you how to code more than one repetitive phrase so that WordStar can insert the appropriate phrase on demand.

WHAT YOU WILL DO

If you have only one phrase that appears frequently in a document, this application is for you! You will begin by opening a document file. Once you have entered WordStar's edit mode, you will start typing your document. The first time you need to use your special word or phrase, you will establish your mini-glossary using WordStar's command ^QA. Then you will use the command ^L whenever you want WordStar to fill in your phrase at the current cursor location.

HOW TO CREATE AND USE A MINI-GLOSSARY

	WordStar Comments and Important Notes	*You Enter . . .*
1	When the no-file menu is displayed on the screen, tell WordStar you want to create or edit a document.	D
2	WordStar asks: NAME OF FILE TO EDIT? WordStar flashes NEW FILE, then transports you to the edit mode.	ANNOUNCE.MEM (Press RETURN.)
3	When the edit-mode main menu appears on the screen, enter the text. Press the space bar once after typing the last word. Do not press RETURN after entering the space.	(Enter text.) The Ecumenical Society to Cover All Possible Eventu-alities, known as
4	This is the first time you are going to use your special word, so tell WordStar you are going to need help inserting a word.	^QA

HOW TO CREATE AND USE A MINI-GLOSSARY

You Enter . . .	*WordStar Comments and Important Notes*	
(Press RETURN.)	WordStar asks: FIND? You do not want to look for anything; you just want to use WordStar's replace capability to insert your special word.	5
ESCAPE (Press RETURN.)	WordStar asks: REPLACE WITH?	6
? (Press RETURN.)	WordStar asks: OPTIONS? (? FOR INFO)	7
N (Press RETURN.)	WordStar provides a choice of options. You choose option N—you only want WordStar to replace your word once without asking. Thereafter, you want to tell WordStar as you go along where to put your repetitive word. Did you see what happened? WordStar added the word ESCAPE after the last space you entered in the text.	8
(Compare texts.)	Now your text should read: The Ecumenical Society to Cover All Possible Eventualities, known as ESCAPE	9

HOW TO CREATE AND USE A MINI-GLOSSARY

WordStar Comments and Important Notes	*You Enter . . .*
10 From now on, any time you want to use the word ESCAPE you can reactivate the replace function by using the command ^L. Enter the rest of the text you see on the next page. Wherever you see the code ^L enter that command to insert the word ESCAPE.	(Enter the text you see at the top of the next page. Use the command ^L as necessary.)
11 If you correctly implemented Word-Star's replace function, your finished document should look like the one at the bottom of the next page.	(Compare documents.)

```
The Ecumenical Society to Cover All Possible Eventualities, known
as ESCAPE, has an offer that may change your life!

^L was established to study the lifestyle alternatives offered by
space  exploration.    Our first commercial colonization  venture
departs  July 4,  1984,  for planets unknown,  with  intermediate
stops on Mars,  Jupiter,  and Uranus.   ^L is the first nonprofit
organization  to  charter  space on the USS  Orwell,  the luxury
flagship of newly incorporated Space-Warp Airways.   You could be
on board, if you become a member of ^L.

Join ^L by dropping by our next membership meeting, to be held at
the Seattle Space Needle restaurant on September 15,  1983.  No-
host  cocktails  will be offered from 1700 to  1900  local  time,
followed  by a review of the ^L charter and a discussion of those
physical,  intellectual,  and financial requirements necessary to
be come an ^List.

Join  ^L,  and become a member of the world's most exclusive  jet
set.
```

```
The Ecumenical Society to Cover All Possible Eventualities, known
as ESCAPE, has an offer that may change your life!

ESCAPE  was  established  to  study  the  lifestyle  alternatives
offered by space exploration.   Our first commercial colonization
venture  departs  July  4,   1984,   for  planets  unknown,  with
intermediate stops on Mars,  Jupiter,  and Uranus. ESCAPE is the
first nonprofit organization to charter space on the USS  Orwell,
the  luxury  flagship of newly incorporated  Space-Warp  Airways.
You could be on board, if you become a member of ESCAPE.

Join  ESCAPE  by dropping by our next membership meeting,  to  be
held  at  the Seattle Space Needle restaurant  on  September  15,
1983.   No-host cocktails will be offered from 1700 to 1900 local
time, followed by a review of the ESCAPE charter and a discussion
of  those  physical,  intellectual,  and  financial  requirements
necessary to be come an ESCAPEist.

Join  ESCAPE,  and become a member of the world's most  exclusive
jet set.
```

HOW TO CREATE AND USE A MINI-GLOSSARY

	WordStar Comments and Important Notes	*You Enter . . .*
12	Now correct any errors. If you find that there is no space between the word ESCAPE and the previous word, you forgot to press the space bar after typing the previous word and before implementing the ^ L command. If you find that the word ESCAPE runs into the word following it, you forgot to press the space bar after implementing the ^ L command and before typing the next word.	(Correct errors using WordStar editing commands.)
13	Once you have corrected your errors, it is time to tell WordStar to save the file. Having saved the document, WordStar will return you to the no-file menu to make another selection.	^KD
14	If you like, you can print this file to see what it looks like on paper.	(Turn on printer. Insert paper.) P
15	WordStar asks: NAME OF FILE TO PRINT? Your printer then types out the meeting announcement.	ANNOUNCE.MEM (Press ESC.)

WHAT YOU JUST DID

You have just used WordStar's search and replace capability in an unusual way to save yourself typing time—and that is really the purpose of word processing. Whenever there is one word or phrase you want to insert in many different places in a document, follow these steps:

1. Begin typing your document. The first time you want to use your special phrase, make sure you enter a blank space after the last word typed, then enter the command ^ QA.
2. Press RETURN when WordStar asks for the word you want to find. This tells WordStar that you do not really want to find a word, you just want to use its replace capability to insert a special phrase.
3. When WordStar asks for the word you want to replace, type your special phrase, then press RETURN.
4. Enter N when WordStar asks you to select an option. That selection ensures that WordStar will insert your special phrase without asking you to confirm your decision. Once you select the option and press RETURN, WordStar will automatically type out your special phrase at the current location of the cursor.
5. Then continue typing your document. Whenever you want to insert your special phrase, enter the command ^ L to repeat the replacement function.

#
3
%
^
6
&
7
*
8
E
Y
S
D
F
H
J
C
V
B
N

six

Form Documents

WHAT IS A FORM DOCUMENT?

A form document is reproduced regularly for many different people or situations. Most of the text is unchanged from situation to situation, with only a few special terms or names changing each time to customize the document.

WHEN TO USE A FORM DOCUMENT

Many finance agreements, lease/rental agreements, and business contracts are really form documents. Before the invention of word processing, the names of the *party of the first part* and the *party of the second part* were typed in blank spaces in the first paragraph of a preprinted document, so that the whole document did not have to be retyped each time in order to insert both names wherever they should appear.

Now, through the magic of word processing, you can customize a whole contract without having to retype standard information. If you find yourself typing a lot of fill-in-the-blank documents, in which you only change names, dates, or dollar amounts, use WordStar to help you develop a form document that can be modified in a few minutes each time you need it.

WHAT YOU WILL DO

First you will create the form document by typing, editing, and saving all the information that will not change from copy to copy. Rather than filling in the blanks with information specific to one client, you will type a special symbol wherever that specific information should appear. WordStar will find and replace each symbol with specific client information each time you print the document for a different person.

Once you have created your form document, we will lead you through the steps necessary to customize it for a particular client. Although a flight contract between a chartering organization and an airline is used as an example, you will see how easy it is to adapt the technique to any other standard document.

HOW TO CREATE A FORM DOCUMENT

WordStar Comments and Important Notes	***You Enter . . .***
1 When the no-file menu is displayed on the screen, tell WordStar you want to create or edit a document.	D
2 WordStar asks: NAME OF FILE TO EDIT? WordStar flashes NEW FILE, then transports you to the edit mode.	CONTRACT.AIR (Press RETURN.)
3 When the edit-mode main menu appears on the screen, enter the text of the document you see on the next page. Be sure to type the document exactly as you see it. This document was typed using the standard margin settings built into WordStar (left margin: column 1; right margin: column 65).	(Enter text.)

```
THIS  AGREEMENT IS ENTERED INTO by the carrier,  herein described
as *, and the chartering organization, herein described as #.

The  carrier,  *,  agrees  to abide by the applicable  rules  and
regulations established by the International Aerospace Consortium
of  1983  in the operation of the described  flight.

*  further  agrees to reserve 15 passenger seats for the  express
use  of passengers approved and contracted by  #.    *  guarantees
that  these  seats  include  life-support  equipment  capable  of
sustaining  passenger  viability  for a minimum of  6  months  at
sublight speeds.

When   assigning  these  seats,   #  ensures  that  all  ticketed
passengers have met or exceeded the Minimum Physical Requirements
for Passengers Attempting Extended Space Travel,  as outlined  in
IAC regulation 14.2.1a.

*  undertakes  to use its best efforts to carry # passengers  and
baggage with reasonable dispatch.   Times shown in timetables  or
elsewhere are not guaranteed,  and form no part of this contract.
Return passage is not guaranteed.  By accepting this Agreement, #
confirms   that  it  will  present  approved  waivers  from   all
passengers  indicating  their  understanding of these  terms  and
resigning all rights to litigation by themselves and their  heirs
in  the  event  that  * is unable to complete  the  flight  in  a
satisfactory manner.
```

You Enter . . .	***WordStar Comments and Important Notes***
.OP (Press RETURN.)	**4** After the last line of text, use the dot command .OP to tell WordStar to omit page numbers when the document is printed. This command must be entered on a line by itself, with the period entered in column 1. There must be no spaces within the command. Complete the command by pressing RETURN after typing the P.

HOW TO CREATE A FORM DOCUMENT

WordStar Comments and Important Notes	*You Enter . . .*
5 All done? Make sure you have corrected any errors.	(Use main-menu commands to correct errors.)
6 Once you have a perfect copy of the document, save it on the disk. Having saved the document, WordStar returns you to the no-file menu to make another selection.	^ KD

HOW TO CUSTOMIZE A FORM DOCUMENT

You Enter . . .	*WordStar Comments and Important Notes*	
D	When the no-file menu is displayed on the screen, tell WordStar you want to create or edit a document.	1
ESCAPE.CNT (Press RETURN.)	WordStar asks: NAME OF FILE TO EDIT? WordStar flashes NEW FILE, then transports you to the edit mode.	2
^ KR	When the edit-mode main menu appears on the screen, tell WordStar to make a copy of the form document you just created, so that you can customize it.	3
CONTRACT.AIR (Press RETURN.)	WordStar asks: NAME OF FILE TO READ? What you see is a copy of your form document. No matter how much you change this copy, which you have named ESCAPE.CNT, your original document, CONTRACT.AIR, will remain unchanged on the disk.	4
(Use cursor-movement commands as necessary.)	Make sure that the cursor is located at the very beginning of the document.	5

HOW TO CUSTOMIZE A FORM DOCUMENT

	WordStar Comments and Important Notes	*You Enter . . .*
6	Now tell WordStar to start customizing the document for SPACE-WARP, the carrier, and ESCAPE, the chartering organization.	^ QA
7	WordStar asks: FIND?	* (Press RETURN.)
8	WordStar asks: REPLACE WITH?	SPACE-WARP (Press RETURN.)
9	WordStar asks: OPTIONS? (? FOR INFO)	? (Press RETURN.)
10	When WordStar lists your options, select N so WordStar will replace without stopping to confirm each change and G so that it will replace throughout the document (globally). Watch WordStar go! It passes through the entire file, looking for every * and replacing each with SPACE-WARP. When WordStar has checked the entire file, it stops at the bottom of the document and waits for further instructions. Don't worry about bringing the cursor back to the beginning—there is a trick for that, as you will see.	NG (Press RETURN.)

HOW TO CUSTOMIZE A FORM DOCUMENT

You Enter . . .	*WordStar Comments and Important Notes*	
^QA	Now you need to replace the symbol # .	**11**
# (Press RETURN.)	WordStar asks: FIND?	**12**
ESCAPE (Press RETURN.)	WordStar asks: REPLACE WITH?	**13**
GNB (Press RETURN.)	WordStar asks: OPTIONS? (? FOR INFO) You don't have to enter ? if you remember what all the options are. You can enter the options right away. This time, select G for global search, N to replace without stopping to confirm each change, and B to search backwards (the trick we mentioned) because the cursor is at the bottom of the document. There it goes again! WordStar looks for and replaces every appearance of the symbol #, ending up with the cursor at the top of the document. As you can see, the document is pushed all out of shape when you insert whole words in place of the single-character symbols. You need to reformat the document to conform to your margin settings.	**14**

HOW TO CUSTOMIZE A FORM DOCUMENT

WordStar Comments and Important Notes	*You Enter . . .*
15 First you want to turn OFF hyphen-help so that WordStar will reformat the entire document without stopping to ask where you would like it to hyphenate a word. Now you are ready to reformat your document. You could reformat one paragraph at a time by using the command ^ B. However, the whole document has to be realigned, so why not use a repeating command?	^ OH
16 Tell WordStar to reformat the whole document. The command ^ QQ will repeat the next command you enter over and over until WordStar reaches the end of the document or you press the space bar to interrupt the process. It is very important that you enter ^ B and not just B. If you do not use the control key when you type the command, you are telling WordStar to print the letter B over and over again! If this happens, stop the repeating command by pressing the space bar. Delete all the B's, move the cursor back to the beginning of the document, and re-enter the command ^ QQ ^ B.	^ QQ ^ B

HOW TO CUSTOMIZE A FORM DOCUMENT

You Enter . . .	*WordStar Comments and Important Notes*	
^ KD	When WordStar stops at the bottom of the document, save it on disk.	**17**
(Turn on printer. Insert paper.) P	When the no-file menu appears on the screen, you are ready to print your new document to see if you did everything correctly.	**18**
ESCAPE.CNT (Press ESC.)	WordStar asks: NAME OF FILE TO PRINT? Your printer immediately begins typing the customized version of your form document.	**19**
(Compare documents.)	If you did everything correctly, your printed copy should look like the one on the next page.	**20**

```
THIS AGREEMENT IS ENTERED INTO by the carrier, herein described
as SPACE-WARP, and the chartering organization, herein described
as ESCAPE.

The carrier, SPACE-WARP, agrees to abide by the applicable rules
and regulations established by the International Aerospace
Consortium of 1983 in the operation of the described flight.

SPACE-WARP further agrees to reserve 15 passenger seats for the
express use of passengers approved and contracted by ESCAPE.
SPACE-WARP guarantees that these seats include life-support
equipment capable of sustaining passenger viability for a minimum
of 6 months at sublight speeds.

When assigning these seats, ESCAPE ensures that all ticketed
passengers have met or exceeded the Minimum Physical Requirements
for Passengers Attempting Extended Space Travel, as outlined in
IAC regulation 14.2.1a.

SPACE-WARP undertakes to use its best efforts to carry ESCAPE
passengers and baggage with reasonable dispatch. Times shown in
timetables or elsewhere are not guaranteed, and form no part of
this contract. Return passage is not guaranteed. By accepting
this Agreement, ESCAPE confirms that it will present approved
waivers from all passengers indicating their understanding of
these terms and resigning all rights to litigation by themselves
and their heirs in the event that SPACE-WARP is unable to
complete the flight in a satisfactory manner.
```

WHAT YOU JUST DID

Congratulations! You have just created your first customized form document. By using the command ^KR to make a copy of the document file rather than modifying the original, you ensured that the form document is always available in its original format, including the variable symbols you inserted.

Practice creating other form documents, using something applicable to your own business. Remember the steps:

1. Create the form document, inserting variable symbols rather than names or dates wherever this information is normally entered. Make sure that the symbols you select are not ones that are used within the standard text of the document, because WordStar cannot tell the difference between symbols you want to change and symbols you want to leave as

they are. You might want to avoid using symbols like $ or % as variables if they are symbols you commonly type as part of the text.

2. Save the form document.
3. Open a new file, using a different file name.
4. Use the command ^KR to read a copy of your form document into the new file.
5. Customize the new file, using WordStar's search and replace command ^QA.
6. Reformat the document using the command ^B or ^QQ^B. If you have included signature blocks or other indented information that should not be reformatted, use the ^B command to reformat one paragraph at a time, to make sure that WordStar does not change any unusually formatted text.
7. Save the customized document.
8. Print the customized document.
9. Create as many customized versions as you want, always beginning by opening a new file and assigning a unique file name. Never, never, never use the name of your form-document file, unless you want to make permanent changes to it.

#
3
%
^
6
&
7
*
8
E
Y
S
D
F
H
J
C
V
B
N

seven

Form Letters and Envelopes

WHAT IS A FORM LETTER?

Some people call it junk mail—but it is a legitimate business practice to send the same letter to many different people so that you can give all of them the same information. A form letter is similar to a form document in that the body of the letter never changes. You simply add the addressee's name and address to the letter in order to customize it.

WHEN TO USE A FORM LETTER

Many companies include a standard cover letter with company literature requested by a potential client. Some sales people follow up a sales call by immediately sending a letter to the customer thanking him or her for the opportunity to visit. Some personnel offices send a standard letter to every individual who sends a resume, confirming that the information will be kept on file for future reference. You can probably think of many occasions in your personal or business life when a form letter would be an appropriate response to an inquiry. This particular application is for those occasions when you want to send less than ten form letters, and do not own or choose to use MailMerge to print multiple copies of the same letter. In *Part Three: MailMerge Applications,* we will show you how MailMerge can automatically insert into a form letter individual names that are stored in a computerized mailing list.

If you want to send a lot of form letters, let MailMerge do all the hard work for you. If you want to send one or two form letters, it can be easier to use WordStar's built-in capabilities to print them. And this exercise will teach you how.

WHAT YOU WILL DO

First, you will create a file that contains only the body of the form letter and a special envelope format. You will use a special symbol to mark the location of the name and address for both the letter and the envelope, just as you did when you created the form document. You will save the form letter and envelope format, open a new document file, and read into it copies of the letter and envelope that you will customize—again, just as you did with the form document.

For each customized letter, you will enter the name and address at the appropriate location. Next, you will copy that address block for the envelope. Finally, you will print the customized letter with the matching envelope.

HOW TO CREATE A FORM LETTER AND ENVELOPE

WordStar Comments and Important Notes	***You Enter . . .***
1 When the no-file menu is displayed on the screen, tell WordStar you want to create or edit a document.	D
2 WordStar asks: NAME OF FILE TO EDIT? WordStar flashes NEW FILE, then transports you to the edit mode.	INQUIRY.LTR (Press RETURN.)

HOW TO CREATE A FORM LETTER AND ENVELOPE

You Enter . . .	***WordStar Comments and Important Notes***
(Enter text.)	**3** When the edit-mode main menu appears on the screen, enter the text of the document you see on the next page. Be sure to type the document exactly as you see it. This document was typed using the standard margin settings built into WordStar (left margin: column 1, right margin: column 65). Notice the command .OP entered at the beginning of the document. As soon as WordStar encounters that, it will know that it should omit page numbers for both the letter and the envelope. Also notice that the dot command .PA is inserted between the letter and the envelope. As soon as you give this command, WordStar will draw a line across the screen to show you that it knows that the command marks the end of one page and the beginning of the next. Both these commands must be typed on lines by themselves, with the period entered in column 1. There must be no spaces within either command. After typing each command, complete it by pressing RETURN.

```
.OP
                                  *


*

Dear *:

Thank you for applying for a seat on ESCAPE's first space flight.

Enclosed  you will find all the necessary documents  required  by
Space-Warp  Airways  and the International Aerospace  Consortium.
These forms must be completed and returned by January 1, 1984, in
order  for  you  to be eligible for consideration.   Be  sure  to
follow the instructions outlined in the attached 350-page guide.

In particular, please be sure your personal therapist  completes
the  orange  psychological-profile form,  listing all  known  and
suspected neuroses, psychoses, and possible paranoid fantasies.

Also be sure that all your former employers,  family members, and
friends complete the compatibility questionnaires.  These will be
used  to  ensure  that all 15 of our passengers  are  capable  of
creating  and  sustaining a pleasant and  productive  environment
during our travel through time and space.

ESCAPE  looks forward to welcoming you aboard our first flight to
the stars.

                                     Sincerely,


                                     Spock Rogers
                                     Quality Control Specialist


Enclosure

.PA

                                  *
```

HOW TO CREATE A FORM LETTER AND ENVELOPE

You Enter . . .	*WordStar Comments and Important Notes*	
(Use main-menu commands to correct errors.)	All done? Make sure you have corrected any errors.	**4**
^ KD	Once you have a perfect copy of the document, save it on disk. Having saved the document, you will be returned to the no-file menu to make another selection.	**5**

HOW TO CUSTOMIZE A FORM LETTER AND ENVELOPE

WordStar Comments and Important Notes	*You Enter . . .*
1 When the no-file menu is displayed on the screen, tell WordStar you want to create or edit a document.	D
2 WordStar asks: NAME OF FILE TO EDIT? WordStar flashes NEW FILE, then transports you to the edit mode.	BUCK.INQ (Press RETURN.)
3 When the edit-mode main menu appears on the screen, tell WordStar to make a copy of the form letter and envelope you have just created, so that you can customize them.	^ KR
4 WordStar asks: NAME OF FILE TO READ? What you see is a copy of your form letter. No matter how much you change this copy, which you have named BUCK.INQ, your original letter, INQUIRY.LTR, will remain unchanged on the disk. Now you are going to customize the letter by inserting the date, name and address, and salutation.	INQUIRY.LTR (Press RETURN.)

HOW TO CUSTOMIZE A FORM LETTER AND ENVELOPE

You Enter . . .	*WordStar Comments and Important Notes*	
^ V (If necessary.)	First, make sure that INSERT is turned ON. Check the right half of the top screen line to see if the comment INSERT ON is displayed. If it is, you are in great shape; do nothing. If not, turn INSERT ON using ^ V.	5
(Use cursor-movement commands as necessary.)	Make sure that the cursor is located at the very beginning of the document.	6
^ QA	Now tell WordStar to start customizing the letter for Mr. Buck. Because each * requires a different item of information, you want WordStar to find each *, replace it with a blank, and then wait for you to type in whatever is appropriate.	7
* (Press RETURN.)	WordStar asks: FIND?	8
(Press RETURN.)	WordStar asks: REPLACE WITH?	9
? (Press RETURN.)	WordStar asks: OPTIONS? (? FOR INFO)	10

HOW TO CUSTOMIZE A FORM LETTER AND ENVELOPE

	WordStar Comments and Important Notes	***You Enter . . .***
11	Word-Star lists your options. WordStar finds the first *, erases it, then stops.	N (Press RETURN.)
12	This is where you type the date. Do not press RETURN after typing the date. Use the command ^ L to tell WordStar to find the next *.	November 14, 1983 ^ L
13	This is where you type Mr. Buck's name and address. Because you want to copy this address block for the envelope, start the first line with the command to mark the beginning of a block.	^ KB Mr. F. Buck (Press RETURN.)
14	Next enter the street address.	100 Outback Way (Press RETURN.)
15	Now enter the city, state, and zip code. After typing the zip code, enter the command to mark the end of a block, then use the command ^ L to tell Word-Star to find the next *.	Bangor, ME 04401 ^ KK ^ L

HOW TO CUSTOMIZE A FORM LETTER AND ENVELOPE

You Enter . . .	*WordStar Comments and Important Notes*	
Foley ^ L	WordStar moves to the salutation so you can enter Mr. Buck's first name. After typing his name, use the command ^ L to tell WordStar to find the next *. Now you are at the right place to enter the address for the envelope. You want to copy the address at the top of the letter, which you marked with beginning and ending block markers, in this location.	**16**
^ KN	First, tell WordStar to use the column-move mode, rather than the normal block-move mode, so that the address lines up properly on the envelope.	**17**
^ KC	Next, give the command to copy the marked address block on the envelope.	**18**

HOW TO CUSTOMIZE A FORM LETTER AND ENVELOPE

WordStar Comments and Important Notes	*You Enter . . .*
19 Now it is time to hide the block markers. When you give the command ^ KH, the block markers you set for the address will disappear from the screen. Once you have hidden the block markers from view, nothing awful will happen if you accidentally type a block command. If you do not hide the block markers, WordStar will carry out any unintentional block command you type.	^ KH
20 It is also a good idea to turn off the column-move mode when you have finished using it, so that the block-move commands will work normally next time you use them.	^ KN
21 You are now ready to save this letter and envelope. If you wanted to create more than one letter at a time, you could now move the cursor to the next blank page using .PA (see *How to Create a Form Letter and Envelope,* instruction 3), read in another copy of your form letter and envelope, and customize this copy for another client, following the steps outlined above. However, for this exercise, we will just save and print this one letter.	^ KD

HOW TO CUSTOMIZE A FORM LETTER AND ENVELOPE

You Enter . . .	*WordStar Comments and Important Notes*	
P	When the no-file menu appears on the screen, you are ready to print the letter and envelope to see if you did everything correctly.	**22**
BUCK.INQ (Press RETURN.)	WordStar asks: NAME OF FILE TO PRINT? Notice that because you want to give further instructions to WordStar, you press RETURN instead of ESC.	**23**
(Press RETURN.)	WordStar asks: DISK FILE OUTPUT	**24**
(Press RETURN.)	WordStar asks: START AT PAGE NUMBER	**25**
(Press RETURN.)	WordStar asks: STOP AFTER PAGE NUMBER	**26**
(Press RETURN.)	WordStar asks: USE FORM FEEDS	**27**
(Press RETURN.)	WordStar asks: SUPPRESS PAGE FORMATTING	**28**

HOW TO CUSTOMIZE A FORM LETTER AND ENVELOPE

	WordStar Comments and Important Notes	*You Enter . . .*
29	WordStar asks: PAUSE FOR PAPER CHANGE BETWEEN PAGES	Y (Press RETURN.)
30	WordStar advises: Ready printer, press RETURN. WordStar begins printing your letter. Notice that the no-file menu command P now reads P STOP PRINT.	(Turn on printer. Insert paper. Press RETURN.)
31	After it has printed the letter, WordStar pauses so that you can insert an envelope. Notice that the P command now reads P CONTINUE PRINT. WordStar now prints your envelope. It may take you a couple of tries to learn how to align the envelope so that the address is properly printed. If it did not print correctly the first time, go through the P command question and answer sequence again, but this time tell WordStar to START at page number 2 (see instruction 25), which is your envelope.	(Remove typed letter. Insert envelope, aligning it so that the print head is about three lines below the top of the envelope.) P
32	When printed properly, your letter and envelope should look like the one on the next page.	(Compare documents.)

November 14, 1983

Mr. F. Buck
100 Outback Way
Bangor, ME 04401

Dear Foley:

Thank you for applying for a seat on ESCAPE's first space flight.

Enclosed you will find all the necessary documents required by Space-Warp Airways and the International Aerospace Consortium. These forms must be completed and returned by January 1, 1984 in order for you to be eligible for consideration. Be sure to follow the instructions outlined in the attached 350-page guide.

In particular, please be sure your personal therapist completes the orange psychological-profile form, listing all known and suspected neuroses, psychoses, and possible paranoid fantasies.

Also be sure that all your former employers, family members, and friends complete the compatibility questionnaires. These will be used to ensure that all 15 of our passengers are capable of creating and sustaining a pleasant and productive environment during our travel through time and space.

ESCAPE looks forward to welcoming you aboard our first flight to the stars.

Sincerely,

Spock Rogers
Quality Control Specialist

Enclosure

Mr. F. Buck
100 Outback Way
Bangor, ME 04401

WHAT YOU JUST DID

Using a few tricky WordStar commands, you have cut your response time to customers at least in half. As you probably realize, you would not want to use this technique if you had to prepare 30 or 40 form letters. However, if you do not own MailMerge or if you just want to send out a few form letters, this WordStar application will help you get them out quickly. Follow these steps:

1. Type your form letter. Wherever variable information is going to appear (date, inside address, salutation), enter an * instead. Be sure to leave only one blank line between the * for the inside address and the word *Dear.* With INSERT ON, the Dear will automatically be pushed down to preserve proper spacing as you type in the address.
2. After typing the form letter, enter the dot command .PA to separate the letter from the envelope address.
3. Type an * where you want the first character in the envelope address to appear.
4. Save this form letter and envelope.
5. Open a new file, using a new file name. Use the command ^ KR to read a copy of your form letter into the new file.
6. Make sure INSERT is ON.
7. Use the command ^ QA, tell WordStar to find the first *, and press RETURN to tell it to replace the * it with a blank.
8. Type in the appropriate information, then enter the command ^ L to ask WordStar to find the next *.
9. Remember to mark the beginning and end of the inside address so that you can copy it to the envelope.
10. When you reach the envelope, use ^ KN to make sure you are in column-move mode, then ^ KC to copy the inside address onto the envelope.
11. Save and print the customized letter and envelope.

That's all there is to it!

If you want to try creating the same letter using MailMerge commands, save the form letter and envelope (INQUIRY.LTR) from this exercise. In *Part Three: MailMerge Applications,* we will show you how to add MailMerge commands to the form letter so that you can see the difference between using WordStar alone and WordStar with MailMerge to generate form letters and envelopes.

#
3
%
ˆ
6
&
7
*
8
E
Y
S
D
F
H
J
C
V
B
N

eight

Boilerplate Paragraphs

WHAT IS A BOILERPLATE PARAGRAPH?

If you have used the old cut-and-paste technique to avoid typing the same text over and over again, you have a good idea what a boilerplate paragraph is. Boilerplate paragraphs are standardized portions of text that are inserted in different locations in many different documents. In general, a boilerplate paragraph contains information that is applicable without change to many different situations.

WHEN TO USE BOILERPLATE PARAGRAPHS

If you work in a customer-service department and spend all day responding to similar letters of complaint and praise from many different customers, you have a perfect application for boilerplate paragraphs. You can use the techniques you will learn here to create a catalog of standard paragraphs that can be mixed and matched to suit almost any situation.

If your correspondence is signed by one of several people, you can use boilerplate techniques to insert the appropriate signature block at the end of each letter. If your firm has developed some legally acceptable terminology that is included in every contract or bid you type, you can create standard paragraphs that can be inserted in every document.

No matter how carefully you word boilerplate paragraphs, no matter how much you try to make them applicable to every situation, sometimes you will have to modify them to respond to particularly confused or peculiar requests or other unusual circumstances. No problem! Once you tell WordStar to read copies of the standard text into a new file, you can edit boilerplate paragraphs any way you like. So boilerplate paragraphs will still save time even if the documents you type often have slight variations.

WHAT YOU WILL DO

First you will create a numbered master list of the paragraphs you want to use on a regular basis. You will transfer each paragraph into its own file so that you can recall each separately. Then you will mix and match these paragraphs to create a couple of different letters. Finally, you will create a new letter, changing the margins so that it will take up more space on the page, and then reading in boilerplate paragraphs and modifying them to respond to an unusual situation.

HOW TO CREATE A MASTER LIST OF BOILERPLATE PARAGRAPHS

	WordStar Comments and Important Notes	***You Enter . . .***
1	When the no-file menu appears on the screen, tell WordStar you want to create or edit a document.	D
2	WordStar asks: NAME OF FILE TO EDIT?	MASTER.PAR (Press RETURN.)
3	When the edit-mode main menu appears on the screen, enter the paragraphs you see on the next page. Be sure to type the numbers and paragraphs exactly as you see them.	(Enter paragraphs.)

1

We are pleased to advise that you have passed our preliminary evaluation for a seat on the USS Orwell.

2

We regret to advise that we will be unable to reserve a seat for you on our first flight aboard the USS Orwell.

3

Please complete the enclosed forms and attach a cashier's check made payable to ESCAPE in the amount of $100,000. Should you be approved for travel, this check is a 10 percent deposit on your reserved seat.

4

Unfortunately, the report received from your therapist indicated that you have experienced, or will experience significant psychological trauma that might make it unwise for you to participate in space travel.

5

Unfortunately, the questionnaires completed by your employers, family members, and friends indicated that it is not possible for you to maintain civil relations with most of the people with whom you come in contact on a regular basis.

6

We eagerly await your check and completed forms, and look forward to strapping you in on July 4, 1984.

7

We will be happy to reconsider your application if you can provide additional material proving the above claims untrue. Simply complete the enclosed 14 forms and attach a check for $1,000 to cover reprocessing costs.

8

Sincerely,

Spock Rogers
Quality Control Specialist

HOW TO CREATE A MASTER LIST OF BOILERPLATE PARAGRAPHS

WordStar Comments and Important Notes	*You Enter . . .*
4 Proofread your paragraphs and correct as necessary. Make sure that the paragraphs are properly numbered, with a blank line between each paragraph and the next number, and between the number and its paragraph.	(Use main-menu commands to correct errors.)
5 Move the cursor back to the beginning of the document so you can start storing your boilerplate paragraphs in individual files.	^ QR
6 Position the cursor on the letter *W* of the word *We* at the beginning of the first paragraph.	(Use cursor-movement commands as necessary.)
7 Mark the beginning of this paragraph. You might see <B>, the beginning block marker, appear.	^ KB
8 Position the cursor on the number *2*, which numbers the second paragraph. You position the cursor there, instead of at the end of the first paragraph, because you want to save both the first paragraph and the carriage return that follows it.	(Use cursor-movement commands as necessary.)

HOW TO CREATE A MASTER LIST OF BOILERPLATE PARAGRAPHS

You Enter . . .	*WordStar Comments and Important Notes*	
^ KK	Mark the end of the paragraph. On some video displays, the ending block marker <K> will appear. On other displays, the whole marked block of text will change intensity. WordStar uses whatever video capabilities are available to highlight a marked section of text visually.	**9**
^ KW	Now you want to save this paragraph in its own file.	**10**
1 (Press RETURN.)	Word-Star asks: NAME OF FILE TO WRITE MARKED TEXT ON? Paragraph 1 is now stored in a separate file.	**11**
^ KH	Now you must hide the block markers so you can mark a new paragraph.	**12**
(Use cursor-movement commands as necessary.)	Position the cursor on the letter *W* of the word *We* at the beginning of the second paragraph.	**13**

HOW TO CREATE A MASTER LIST OF BOILERPLATE PARAGRAPHS

WordStar Comments and Important Notes	***You Enter . . .***
14 Mark the beginning of this paragraph. You might see <B>, the beginning block marker, appear.	^ KB
15 Position the cursor on the number *3,* which numbers the third paragraph.	(Use cursor-movement commands as necessary.)
16 Mark the end of the paragraph. The marked block of text will be highlighted in some way (see instruction 9).	^ KK
17 Now save this paragraph in its own file.	^ KW
18 WordStar asks: NAME OF FILE TO WRITE MARKED TEXT ON? Paragraph 2 has now been stored in a separate file.	2 (Press RETURN.)
19 Now hide the block markers so you can mark a new paragraph.	^ KH

HOW TO CREATE A MASTER LIST OF BOILERPLATE PARAGRAPHS

You Enter . . .	*WordStar Comments and Important Notes*	
(Create separate files for paragraphs 3 through 7.)	Do you see what is going on here? Try creating separate files on your own for paragraphs 3 through 7. First, use ^X to move the cursor to the first letter of the first word in a paragraph. Enter the beginning block marker using ^KB. Then move the cursor with ^X so that it covers the number of the following paragraph. Enter the ending block marker using ^KK. Tell WordStar to write a copy of this paragraph to a separate file with ^KW. Then use ^KH to hide the block markers so you can work on the next paragraph. Stop when you reach paragraph 8, which you will handle a little differently. Finished so soon? Good for you! Your cursor should be positioned on the number 8, because you should have just finished storing a copy of paragraph 7.	**20**
(Use cursor-movement commands as necessary.)	Now position the cursor in column 1 of the line that reads *Sincerely,* in paragraph 8.	**21**
^KB	Mark the beginning of this paragraph. You might see <B>, the beginning block marker, appear.	**22**

HOW TO CREATE A MASTER LIST OF BOILERPLATE PARAGRAPHS

	WordStar Comments and Important Notes	***You Enter . . .***
23	Position the cursor in column 1 of the second blank line below *Quality Control Specialist,* at the end of the paragraph 8.	(Use cursor-movement commands as necessary.)
24	Mark the end of the block of text. The marked block of text will be visually highlighted in some way.	^ KK
25	Save this paragraph in its own file.	^ KW
26	WordStar asks: NAME OF FILE TO WRITE MARKED TEXT ON? Paragraph 8 is now stored in a separate file.	8 (Press RETURN.)
27	Although you do not need to set any more block markers, it is good to get in the habit of hiding block markers when you no longer need them.	^ KH
28	You have successfully filed each paragraph under its own file name and can use each one as necessary in a letter. Now store this master file to use as a reference list.	^ KD

HOW TO CREATE A MASTER LIST OF BOILERPLATE PARAGRAPHS

You Enter . . .	*WordStar Comments and Important Notes*	
(Turn on printer. Insert paper.) P	WordStar returns you to the no-file menu. Print your master file so that you have a reference list of your boilerplate paragraphs.	29
MASTER.PAR (Press ESC.)	WordStar asks: NAME OF FILE TO PRINT?	30
(Compare paragraphs.)	Your reference list should look just like the page of paragraphs you typed from page 87, including the numbers.	31

WHAT YOU JUST DID

You have just created a reference list from which you can select boilerplate paragraphs for insertion in letters to different customers. You have also created separate files for a copy of each paragraph, so that you can insert into a letter only those paragraphs that apply to a particular customer. Once you have written your boilerplate paragraphs, this is how you create the reference list file and the individual paragraph files:

1. Open a file for your master list. Enter a *1* in column 1 of the first line of your file. Then press RETURN twice so that there is a blank line between the number 1 and its paragraph. Now type the paragraph.

2. Once you have completed the first paragraph, press RETURN twice so that you leave a blank line between the end of the first paragraph and the number 2. Having typed 2 in column 1, press RETURN twice and type your second paragraph. Continue in this way for all your succeeding paragraphs. This file is your master list.

3. After you have entered and edited all your paragraphs, return to the beginning of the file, using the command ^QR to get there quickly, and begin storing each paragraph in its own file.

4. Position the cursor on the first letter of the first word of the first paragraph and enter ^KB, the beginning block marker command. Then position the cursor on the number of the next paragraph and enter ^KK, the ending block marker command.

5. Store this marked paragraph in its own file by entering the command ^KW and typing the paragraph number as its file name. Follow steps 4 and 5 to store each paragraph in its own file.

6. Once you have stored each paragraph separately, use ^KD to save your master list and P to print a copy of it for reference. Whenever you want to insert a boilerplate paragraph into a letter, you can look up its file number on this list.

Ready to use these boilerplate paragraphs to write a letter? Place your reference list next to your terminal so you can look up the right paragraph numbers, then read on.

HOW TO USE BOILERPLATE PARAGRAPHS

You Enter . . .	*WordStar Comments and Important Notes*	
D	When the no-file menu appears on the screen, tell WordStar you want to create or edit a document.	**1**
ACCEPT.LTR (Press RETURN.)	WordStar asks: NAME OF FILE TO EDIT? WordStar flashes the comment NEW FILE, takes you to the edit mode, and displays the main menu.	**2**
(Enter text.)	First enter the date, name and address, and salutation you see below:	**3**

```
                         July 25, 1983


Mr. C. Pott
1234 Main Street
San Leandro, CA 94578

Dear Mr. Pott:
```

HOW TO USE BOILERPLATE PARAGRAPHS

WordStar Comments and Important Notes	***You Enter . . .***
4 Move the cursor down to the second line below the salutation, where you would normally begin entering the text of the letter.	(Press RETURN as necessary.)
5 Now you want to read a copy of your positive introductory paragraph into the ACCEPT.LTR file, since Mr. Pott is one of the lucky few who made it past ESCAPE's tough initial evaluation.	^ KR
6 WordStar asks: NAME OF FILE TO READ? WordStar inserts a copy of your paragraph that begins *We are pleased to advise.*	1 (Press RETURN.)
7 Notice that the cursor has remained on the first word of the paragraph. You need to move it down to the correct position to read in your next paragraph.	^ QC
8 With the cursor now correctly positioned, tell WordStar to read in the next paragraph you have chosen.	^ KR

HOW TO USE BOILERPLATE PARAGRAPHS

You Enter . . .	*WordStar Comments and Important Notes*	
3 (Press RETURN.)	Word-Star asks: NAME OF FILE TO READ? Paragraph 3 tells the space traveller to fill out more forms and send in a deposit. Lucky Mr. Pott—just a few more forms and he is on his way!	**9**
^ QC	Now move the cursor down to the correct position for the first line of your closing paragraph. Because you included a blank line at the end of each stored paragraph, ^ QC, the command to move the cursor to the end of the document, works just fine.	**10**
^ KR	Tell WordStar you want to read in another paragraph.	**11**
6 (Press RETURN.)	WordStar asks: NAME OF FILE TO READ?	**12**
^ QC	Now you need to move the cursor down to insert the signature block.	**13**

HOW TO USE BOILERPLATE PARAGRAPHS

	WordStar Comments and Important Notes	***You Enter . . .***
14	Tell WordStar to read in another paragraph.	^ KR
15	WordStar asks: NAME OF FILE TO READ?	8 (Press RETURN.)
16	This is a one-page letter, so you do not want WordStar to number this page. Move the cursor to the bottom of the document and include the command .OP to omit page numbering. Remember, this command must be entered on a line by itself. The period must appear in column 1, with no spaces anywhere within the command. Complete the command by pressing RETURN.	.OP (Press RETURN.)
17	Before you save this letter, take a look at it on the screen. (You may have to use scrolling commands.) It should look like the one on the next page.	(Compare letters.)
18	If it all looks good, save the file.	^ KD

```
                              July 25, 1983


Mr. C. Pott
1234 Main Street
San Leandro, CA 94578

Dear Mr. Pott:

We  are  pleased to advise that you have passed  our  preliminary
evaluation for a seat on the USS Orwell.

Please  complete the enclosed forms and attach a cashier's  check
made  payable to ESCAPE in the amount of $100,000.  Should you be
approved for travel,  this check is a 10 percent deposit on  your
reserved seat.

We eagerly await your check and completed forms, and look forward
to strapping you in on July 4, 1984.

                              Sincerely,


                              Spock Rogers
                              Quality Control Specialist


.OP
```

You Enter . . .	*WordStar Comments and Important Notes*	
(Turn on printer. Insert paper.) P	If you want to, you can now print the letter. It should look exactly like the the copy shown above, without the command .OP. When WordStar prints the letter, it acts on this command and omits the page numbering.	**19**

HOW TO USE BOILERPLATE PARAGRAPHS

WordStar Comments and Important Notes	*You Enter . . .*
20 Now try creating a letter rejecting someone's application to ESCAPE. Make up a date and a name and address. Then use paragraph 2, either paragraph 4 or 5, then paragraph 7, and close with signature block 8. Use all the commands you have learned in this exercise to insert the paragraphs in the appropriate places. The rejection letter should look like this:	(Create another letter.)

```
                                   (Date)


(Passenger Name)
(Street Address)
(City, State, Zip)

Dear (Name):

We  regret to advise that we will be unable to reserve a seat for
you on our first flight aboard the USS Orwell.

Unfortunately,  the  questionnaires completed by your  employers,
family members, and friends indicated that it is not possible for
you to maintain civil relations with most of the people with whom
you come in contact on a regular basis.

We  will  be  happy  to reconsider your application  if  you  can
provide  additional  material proving the  above  claims  untrue.
Simply  complete  the  enclosed 14 forms and attach a  check  for
$1,000 to cover reprocessing costs.

                                   Sincerely,


                                   Spock Rogers
                                   Quality Control Specialist
.OP
```

WHAT YOU JUST DID

As you created and used these boilerplate paragraphs, you probably thought of lots of other ways to use this technique. It is worth spending some time analyzing the correspondence and documents you write regularly to see if they lend themselves to this application. Once your boilerplate paragraphs are developed, follow the steps below to use them whenever appropriate:

1. Position the cursor where you want the first character of the boilerplate paragraph to appear.
2. Use the command ^ KR to tell WordStar to make a copy of the boilerplate paragraph at the cursor position.
3. The cursor will still be on the first letter of the paragraph you have inserted, so move it to the end of your document with the command ^ QC.
4. Continue using ^ KR and ^ QC to cut-and-paste your document, typing in additional text as necessary.

If you own MicroPro's MailMerge program, you can use it to merge boilerplate paragraphs. Rather than actually reading copies of your paragraphs into a new document file, you enter merging commands, using the appropriate boilerplate file names, wherever you wanted the paragraphs to appear. You do not see these paragraphs on your video display; they are automatically inserted in the document when it is printed. That is the advantage of using MailMerge for this operation—disk space is not taken up with copies of the original paragraphs because they only appear in the printed version of your customized letter. The disadvantage? You do not see what the document is really going to look like until you print it.

If you do not own MailMerge, or if you need to see or edit the paragraphs before printing the document, you can always follow the steps outlined above. Yes, once you read copies of standard paragraphs into your document file, you can edit them to produce customized versions for individual clients. Because you edit copies of the paragraphs, not the original files, you always have the original files available for reuse. We will show you briefly how to customize in the next part of this exercise.

HOW TO CUSTOMIZE BOILERPLATE PARAGRAPHS

WordStar Comments and Important Notes	*You Enter . . .*
1 When the no-file menu appears on the screen, tell WordStar you want to create or edit a document.	D
2 WordStar asks: NAME OF FILE TO EDIT? WordStar flashes the comment NEW FILE, takes you to the edit mode, and displays the main menu.	SOD.LTR (Press RETURN.)
3 You are going to type a short letter, so you want to set wider margins. First, change the left margin.	^OL
4 WordStar asks: LEFT MARGIN COLUMN NUMBER (ESCAPE for cursor column)? Notice that the ruler line has changed, showing that the left margin is now set at column 5.	5 (Press RETURN.)
5 Now change the right margin.	^OR

HOW TO CUSTOMIZE BOILERPLATE PARAGRAPHS

You Enter . . .	*WordStar Comments and Important Notes*	
55 (Press RETURN.)	WordStar asks: RIGHT MARGIN COLUMN NUMBER (ESCAPE for cursor column)? The ruler line has changed again, showing that the right margin is now set at column 55. Now you are ready to begin typing your letter.	**6**
(Enter text.)	First you must enter the date, the name and address, and the salutation for your letter. Enter the text you see below:	**7**
(Press RETURN as necessary.)	Using the RETURN key, move the cursor down to the second line below the salutation, where you would normally begin entering the text of the body of the letter.	**8**

```
                              January 11, 1984


Mr. D. Sod
5050 Odd Way
Rough and Ready, CA 93894

Dear Mr. Sod:
```

HOW TO CUSTOMIZE BOILERPLATE PARAGRAPHS

	WordStar Comments and Important Notes	***You Enter . . .***
9	Now you want to read in a copy of your negative introductory paragraph, since Mr. Sod is unacceptable as a passenger aboard the USS Orwell.	^ KR
10	WordStar asks: NAME OF FILE TO READ? WordStar has just inserted a copy of your paragraph beginning *We regret to advise.* Notice that the paragraph is wider than your current margin settings. Don't worry about that right now. Once you have made all your editing changes, we will show you how to reformat the paragraphs to fit your new margins.	2 (Press RETURN.)
11	Now move the cursor down to the correct position to read in your next paragraph.	^ QC
12	The cursor is correctly positioned, so read in your next paragraph.	^ KR
13	Word-Star asks: NAME OF FILE TO READ?	4 (Press RETURN.)

HOW TO CUSTOMIZE BOILERPLATE PARAGRAPHS

You Enter . . .	*WordStar Comments and Important Notes*	
^QC	Mr. Sod's case is so unusual that we do not have an apppropriate closing paragraph already prepared. You will have to type in a special one just for him. Move the cursor down to the correct position for the first line of your closing paragraph.	**14**
(Enter paragraph.) Because of the information in the reports cited above, we regret that we will be unable to consider you for any flights sponsored by ESCAPE, now or in the future.	Type in the paragraph as shown.	**15**
(Press RETURN twice.)	Once you have typed the closing paragraph, press RETURN twice to position the cursor properly for the insertion of the signature block.	**16**
^KR	Tell WordStar you want to read in another paragraph.	**17**
8 (Press RETURN.)	WordStar asks: NAME OF FILE TO READ?	**18**

HOW TO CUSTOMIZE BOILERPLATE PARAGRAPHS

	WordStar Comments and Important Notes	*You Enter . . .*
19	This is a one-page letter, so you do not want WordStar to number this page. Move the cursor to the bottom of the document and include the command .OP to omit page numbering. Remember, this command must be entered on a line by itself. The period must appear in column 1, with no spaces anywhere within the command. Complete the command by pressing RETURN.	.OP (Press RETURN.)
20	So far, your letter looks like the one on the next page.	(Compare letters.)

```
                              January 11, 1984


     Mr. D. Sod
     5050 Odd Way
     Rough and Ready, CA 93894

     Dear Mr. Sod:

We  regret to advise that we will be unable to reserve a seat for
you on our first flight aboard the USS Orwell.

Unfortunately,  the report received from your therapist indicated
that  you  have  experienced,   or  will  experience  significant
psychological  trauma  that  might  make it  unwise  for  you  to
participate in space travel.

     Because  of  the information in the  reports  cited
     above, we regret that we will be unable to consider
     you for any flights sponsored by ESCAPE,  now or in
     the future.

                         Sincerely,


                         Spock Rogers
                         Quality Control Specialist

.OP
```

You Enter . . .	*WordStar Comments and Important Notes*	
(Use cursor-movement commands as necessary.)	Obviously you need to reformat your two boilerplate paragraphs to fit your new margins. In addition, you have decided that you want to add a few words to one of them. First, move the cursor to the letter *W* in the first word *We* in the first sentence of the first paragraph.	**21**

HOW TO CUSTOMIZE BOILERPLATE PARAGRAPHS

WordStar Comments and Important Notes	*You Enter . . .*
22 All you want to do to this paragraph is format it to fit within your new margin settings. If hyphen-help is ON, you may have to give the command ^ B several times to make WordStar reformat the whole paragraph without hyphens.	^ B (As necessary.)
23 Now you want to add a few words to the second boilerplate paragraph. Move the cursor until it covers the *o* in the word *or* in the sentence *or will experience.*	(Use cursor-movement commands as necessary.)
24 Check the upper right-hand portion of the status line. If you see the comment INSERT ON, skip this instruction. If the comment is not there, turn INSERT ON.	^ V (If necessary.)
25 With INSERT now ON, type the word *and.* Notice that the word *or* is pushed ahead of your insertion.	and
26 To delete the word *or,* use WordStar's word-delete command.	^ T

HOW TO CUSTOMIZE BOILERPLATE PARAGRAPHS

You Enter . . .	*WordStar Comments and Important Notes*	
^ D (As necessary.)	Now move the cursor to the right until it covers the first letter e in the word *experience* on that same line.	27
continue to (Press space bar once.)	With INSERT still ON, type the words *continue to,* followed by one blank space to separate the insertion from the word that follows it.	28
(Use cursor-movement commands as necessary.)	You have finished editing this paragraph. Move the cursor back up until it covers the first letter in the first word of this paragraph.	29
^ B (As necessary.)	Reformat this paragraph to fit your margin settings. If hyphen-help is ON, you may have to give the command ^ B several times to make WordStar reformat the whole paragraph without hyphens.	30
(Compare letters.)	Your completed letter should look like the one on the next page.	31
^ KD	Everything correct? Save this letter.	32

```
                                        January 11, 1984


          Mr. D. Sod
          5050 Odd Way
          Rough and Ready, CA 93894

          Dear Mr. Sod:

          We   regret   to   advise that we will  be  unable  to
          reserve  a seat for you on our first flight  aboard
          the USS Orwell.

          Unfortunately,    the  report  received  from   your
          therapist indicated that you have experienced,  and
          will    continue    to    experience    significant
          psychological  trauma that might make it unwise for
          you to participate in space travel.

          Because  of  the information in the  reports  cited
          above, we regret that we will be unable to consider
          you for any flights sponsored by ESCAPE,  now or in
          the future.
                                   Sincerely,

                                   Spock Rogers
                                   Quality Control Specialist

       .OP
```

WHAT YOU JUST DID

You have saved time by using boilerplate paragraphs as often as possible, editing as necessary to produce a really customized letter. As you have seen, you can use all WordStar's editing commands to modify a boilerplate paragraph once it has been inserted in a document. WordStar does not care how the paragraph becomes part of your letter or where it comes from—once the paragraph is read into the new file and is displayed on your screen, you can edit it as much as you like.

#
3
^
6
&
7
*
8
E
Y
S
D
F
H
J
C
V
B
N

nine

Variable Margins within a Paragraph

WHAT ARE VARIABLE MARGINS?

Usually, you set margins before you begin writing and that is the way they stay for the whole document. Sometimes, however, you need to change the margins within a paragraph to accommodate a photograph or drawing. If this is the case, you will have to set different margins for each section of the paragraph.

WHEN TO USE VARIABLE MARGINS

If you write company manuals, you may want to print graphs or charts to illustrate the text. If you create sales catalogs, you will need to leave space to paste in a picture of each product next to its description. Sometimes you may want to create unusual formats just to impress your friends.

Using WordStar margin-setting commands, you can vary the margins within a paragraph to leave space for charts or photos, or just to produce an interesting format. Once you have printed a copy of the document, you can paste in the appropriate pictures and duplicate the pages on a photocopy machine or offset printing equipment.

WHAT YOU WILL DO

First you will set the margins for the first line of text you want to type. You will type the whole paragraph to fit within these margins. Then you will reset the margins for your succeeding sections, and reformat only the lines you want to adjust.

HOW TO CREATE VARIABLE MARGINS WITHIN A PARAGRAPH

	WordStar Comments and Important Notes	*You Enter . . .*
1	When the no-file menu is on the screen, tell WordStar you want to create or edit a document.	D
2	WordStar asks: NAME OF FILE TO EDIT? WordStar flashes NEW FILE, then transports you to the edit mode.	BADGE.FRM (Press RETURN.)
3	When the edit-mode main menu appears on the screen, begin by resetting the left margin.	^ OL
4	WordStar asks: LEFT MARGIN COLUMN NUMBER (ESCAPE for cursor column)? Notice that the ruler line has changed to reflect a left margin setting of 10.	10 (Press RETURN.)
5	Now change the right margin.	^ OR

HOW TO CREATE VARIABLE MARGINS WITHIN A PARAGRAPH

	You Enter . . .	*WordStar Comments and Important Notes*
6	35 (Press RETURN.)	WordStar asks: RIGHT MARGIN COLUMN NUMBER (ESCAPE for cursor column)?
7	(Enter text.)	Now the right margin is set at column 35. Type the text you see below. In case you are wondering, you are typing the front of an ESCAPE I.D. badge.

```
HELLO, MY NAME IS:

This   is   to certify   that
the    bearer    of     this
identification    is      a
confirmed passenger aboard
the  USS   Orwell,   flight
date July 4, 1984.  If you
suspect that the bearer of
this   badge   could    not
possibly  be approved   for
extended space travel,  do
not   hesitate  to  compare
the     bearer's    retinal
pattern      with      that
reproduced above.
```

HOW TO CREATE VARIABLE MARGINS WITHIN A PARAGRAPH

	WordStar Comments and Important Notes	*You Enter . . .*
8	Correct any errors.	(Correct as necessary.)
9	Now reset the right margin so you can reformat the bottom half of the text to fit around the retinal pattern that will be reproduced on the badge.	^ OR
10	WordStar asks: RIGHT MARGIN COLUMN NUMBER (ESCAPE for cursor column)?	65 (Press RETURN.)
11	Notice that the right margin has been reset on the ruler line. Now move the cursor until it covers the first letter in the word *this* in the line that reads *this badge could not possibly.*	(Use cursor-movement commands as necessary.)
12	Reformat this line and all following lines by using the WordStar command ^ B. If hyphen-help is turned ON, you may need to enter the command several times to reach the end of the paragraph without hyphenating any words.	^ B (As necessary.)
13	Your paragraph should now look like the one on the next page.	(Compare texts.)

```
HELLO, MY NAME IS:

This  is to  certify  that
the    bearer    of    this
identification     is     a
confirmed passenger aboard
the   USS   ORWELL,   flight
date July 4, 1984.  If you
suspect that the bearer of
this  badge could not possibly be approved for  extended
space  travel, do not hesitate to compare the  bearer's
retinal pattern with that reproduced above.
```

You Enter . . .	WordStar Comments and Important Notes	
(Press RETURN twice.)	Look good? Now type the back of the badge, where ESCAPE wants to insert its logo, a stairway to the stars. Press RETURN twice to move the cursor down to begin typing the text for the back of the badge.	14
^ OL	Leave the right margin at column 65 but reset the left margin for the first line of text in this section.	15
45 (Press RETURN.)	WordStar asks: LEFT MARGIN COLUMN NUMBER (ESCAPE for cursor column)?	16
(Enter text.)	Now enter the text on the next page.	17

```
                                        I promise to abide by
                                        the     rules     and
                                        regulations  of  the
                                        Ecumenical Society to
                                        Cover   All  Possible
                                        Eventualities
                                        (ESCAPE)        while
                                        preparing   for,   in
                                        transit  to,   or  on
                                        board a flight to the
                                        outer limits of man's
                                        imagination.    I  do
                                        solemnly swear that I
                                        am of sound mind  and
                                        body  (as defined  in
                                        ESCAPE's   Guide  for
                                        the     Intergalactic
                                        Traveller),  and will
                                        make every effort  to
                                        remain   so  while  a
                                        registered member  of
                                        ESCAPE.
```

WordStar Comments and Important Notes	***You Enter . . .***
18 Correct any errors.	(Correct as necessary.)
19 Now the fun begins. We want to change the margins every third line to create a stairway effect. First tell WordStar to reset the left margin.	^ OL
20 WordStar asks: LEFT MARGIN COLUMN NUMBER (ESCAPE for cursor column)?	30 (Press RETURN.)

HOW TO CREATE VARIABLE MARGINS WITHIN A PARAGRAPH

You Enter . . .	***WordStar Comments and Important Notes***	
(Use cursor-movement commands as necessary.)	Move the cursor to the first letter in line four, which begins *Ecumenical.*	**21**
^ B (As necessary.)	Tell WordStar to reformat the paragraph beginning with that word. Because your margin settings are so wide, you may have to enter the reformat command several times to get all the way through the paragraph without hyphenating.	**22**
^ OL	Every line except the first three is now formatted with the left margin at column 30. It is time to reset the left margin again.	**23**

HOW TO CREATE VARIABLE MARGINS WITHIN A PARAGRAPH

WordStar Comments and Important Notes	***You Enter . . .***
24 WordStar asks: LEFT MARGIN COLUMN NUMBER (ESCAPE for cursor column)?	15 (Press RETURN.)
25 Now move the cursor until it covers the first letter in line seven which begins with the word *or*.	(Use cursor-movement commands as necessary.)
26 Reformat the paragraph beginning with that word. You may have to enter the command ^ B several times to reach the end of the paragraph without hyphenating.	^ B (As necessary.)
27 Now reset the left margin to position the bottom step.	^ OL
28 WordStar asks: LEFT MARGIN COLUMN NUMBER (ESCAPE for cursor column)?	1 (Press RETURN.)
29 Now that the left margin has been reset, move the cursor until it covers the first letter in line ten, which begins *for the Intergalactic Traveller*.	(Use cursor-movement commands as necessary.)

HOW TO CREATE VARIABLE MARGINS WITHIN A PARAGRAPH

You Enter . . .	*WordStar Comments and Important Notes*	
^ B (As necessary.)	Reformat the rest of the paragraph.	**30**
(Compare texts.)	Pretty flashy! Your paragraph should now look like the one below.	**31**
^ KD	If you want to you can save this file. If you were an ESCAPE employee, you would customize the badges, print them out on your printer, and take them to be offset printed and laminated for your passengers.	**32**

```
                                           I promise to abide by
                                           the      rules     and
                                           regulations   of   the
                           Ecumenical   Society  to  Cover  All
                           Possible   Eventualities   (ESCAPE)
                           while preparing for, in transit  to,
               or  on board a flight to the outer limits of  man's
               imagination. I do solemnly swear that I am of sound
               mind   and  body  (as   defined   in   ESCAPE's  Guide
for the Intergalactic Traveller),  and will make every effort  to
remain so while a registered member of ESCAPE.
```

WHAT YOU JUST DID

You have created a special format that can accommodate a drawing within a paragraph. You have also drawn a picture using text. No matter how sophisticated an operator you are, it will always take a few tries to get your text pictures just right. Luckily, WordStar does not change the text as you change the margins, so you can start all over if you discover you made a complete mess of your paragraph. Here are a few hints to help you create fancy formats:

1. Remember you have to work from top to bottom in a paragraph. Initially set the margins to match the first line of text you enter.
2. Type the whole paragraph to fit these margins.
3. Reset the margins to match the first line of text you want to modify.
4. Place the cursor on the first letter in the first word you want to reformat.
5. Use the reformat command ^B to modify the rest of the paragraph.
6. Working down through the paragraph, continue to reset the margins and reformat the paragraph until it looks just right.

#
3
%
^
6
&
7
*
8
E
Y
S
D
F
H
J
C
V
B
N

ten

Two-column Formats

WHAT IS A TWO-COLUMN FORMAT?

Two-column format is a page layout used in newsletters and magazines. The text is laid out in two narrow columns, with the text starting in the left-hand column and continuing in the right-hand column.

WHEN TO USE A TWO-COLUMN FORMAT

The average business correspondent does not have much use for two-column format. However, people who write newsletters, magazine copy, or advertisement copy often use this format because it is eye-catching and easy to read. The copy is typeset in one long, narrow column and is then cut and pasted up into two-column pages, usually by a graphic artist. If you do not have your newsletter or copy typeset by a professional typesetter, you can use WordStar to create finished two-column formats that can be taken to an offset printer, who will print directly from your original.

WHAT YOU WILL DO

First you will set the margins so that you can type your entire document using a line length that is the width of each column. Since you cannot do any editing once you have the two columns in place on the page, you will correct any errors before you paste up your right-hand column.

Once you are sure the text is correct, you will use WordStar's column-move function, marking the section of text that will end up as your right-hand column and moving it to the appropriate place on the page.

HOW TO CREATE A TWO-COLUMN FORMAT

	WordStar Comments and Important Notes	***You Enter . . .***
1	When the no-file menu appears on the screen, tell WordStar you want to create a new document.	D
2	WordStar asks: NAME OF FILE TO EDIT? WordStar transports you to the edit mode, and displays the main menu on the screen.	LIMITS.CPY (Press RETURN.)
3	The first thing you want to do is reset the right margin for the narrow column of text.	^ OR
4	WordStar asks: RIGHT MARGIN COLUMN NUMBER (ESCAPE for cursor column)? Notice that the ruler line has changed, and that the right margin is now set at column 30.	30 (Press RETURN.)

HOW TO CREATE A TWO-COLUMN FORMAT

You Enter . . .	*WordStar Comments and Important Notes*	
.UJ OFF (Press RETURN.)	Begin by entering the special dot command .UJ OFF, being sure to follow all the rules for correct formatting of dot commands. If you own a letter-quality printer that can microspace justify (add tiny spaces between letters to create even right margins), you must add this command to the top of your document to turn microspace justification off. Otherwise, when you paste up your second column, the unseen tiny spaces between the left- and right-hand columns may push the columns out of alignment, producing a two-column format that wiggles on the page. If you do not own a printer that can microspace justify you will not have this problem, so you do not need to add this special dot command.	**5**
.PO 3 (Press RETURN.)	Next, add the dot command .PO 3, which tells WordStar to start printing at the third column from the left edge of the paper so that two columns will fit on one page.	**6**
(Enter text.)	Now type the text on the next page.	**7**

```
.UJ OFF
.PO 3

EACH   PASSENGER  MUST  CARRY:

A minimum of $100,000 in  cash
or  negotiable  securities  to
cover   incidental  meal   and
medical    expenses    for   the
duration of the flight;

Survival  equipment including,
but    not    limited    to,    a
multipurpose      pen      knife,
canteen, portable oxygen tank,
IAC-approved,   all-atmosphere
tent bag,  and flashlight with
long-life batteries;

No more than 10 lb of luggage,
including      prospecting    and
survival   equipment.   Excess
baggage may be transported  at
the discretion of the carrier,
at    a    fee   of   $1,000    per
additional ounce.

NO PASSENGER MAY CARRY:

Sporting    equipment   of    any
kind,  since  land,  sea,  and
aerial    sports   will   not   be
permitted for the duration  of
the  flight,  and are unlikely
at any planet of destination;

Pets of any  size,  shape,  or
description,  unless the pet's
owner  has paid full fare  for
its transportation;

Arms   or   weapons of any  kind
unless approved by the Captain
or,  in the event of the death
or  permanent   disablement  of
the    Captain   prior   to    the
conclusion of the  flight,  by
another        duly          elected
authority.
```

HOW TO CREATE A TWO-COLUMN FORMAT

You Enter . . .	*WordStar Comments and Important Notes*	
(Edit as necessary.)	Carefully proofread and edit your document. If you have to make corrections, use WordStar's ^ B command to reformat the text to fit within the margins you have set. Once you paste the right-hand column in its proper location on the page, you will not be able to do any more editing. This is because the column-move mode only operates when moving text. When you reformat or edit, WordStar perceives the whole page from left to right margin as one block of text and will try to merge the left- and right-hand columns into one column as you make changes. At this point, you could save this document, print it, and then manually paste up the right-hand column to achieve the two-column look. But why not let WordStar do it for you?	**8**
^ KN	WordStar is normally in the plain block mode, which will move every character between the right and left margins of a marked block of text. The first thing you must do is tell WordStar you want it to use the column-move mode.	**9**

HOW TO CREATE A TWO-COLUMN FORMAT

	WordStar Comments and Important Notes	***You Enter . . .***
10	Now you need to mark the beginning of the right column, which starts with the words *NO PASSENGER*. Position the cursor on the *N* of the word *NO* and enter the beginning block marker.	^ KB
11	Move the cursor to the last line of text in the file, and then move the cursor to column 31 of that line. While using the column-move mode, be sure to include all of the characters in the column. With the right margin set at column 30, you are sure to move everything if you place the cursor in column 31.	(Use cursor-movement commands as necessary.)

HOW TO CREATE A TWO-COLUMN FORMAT

You Enter . . .	*WordStar Comments and Important Notes*	
^KK	When the cursor is properly positioned, enter the ending block marker command.	12
^QR	Now move the cursor back to the beginning of the document.	13
^OR	Change the right margin so you can paste up your right-hand column.	14
70 (Press RETURN.)	WordStar asks: RIGHT MARGIN COLUMN NUMBER (ESCAPE for cursor column)?	15
(Use cursor-movement commands as necessary.)	Now move the cursor to the first line of text in the document, which begins with the words *EACH PASSENGER MUST.* Then move the cursor to column 40 of that same line. This is where the first line of your right-hand column of text should begin. Make sure you are in the right place by checking the top line of the screen display.	16

HOW TO CREATE A TWO-COLUMN FORMAT

	WordStar Comments and Important Notes	*You Enter . . .*
17	Now tell WordStar to paste up your right-hand column by moving the block of text you have just marked.	^ KV
18	Your text should now look like this:	(Compare texts.)

```
.UJ OFF
.PO 3

EACH   PASSENGER  MUST   CARRY:         NO PASSENGER MAY CARRY:

A minimum of $100,000 in  cash          Sporting   equipment  of   any
or  negotiable  securities  to          kind,  since  land,  sea,  and
cover   incidental  meal   and          aerial   sports  will  not  be
medical   expenses   for   the          permitted for the duration  of
duration of the flight;                 the  flight,  and are unlikely
                                        at any planet of destination;
Survival  equipment including,
but   not   limited   to,    a          Pets of any  size,  shape,  or
multipurpose    pen     knife,          description,  unless the pet's
canteen, portable oxygen tank,          owner  has paid full fare  for
IAC-approved,   all-atmosphere          its transportation;
tent bag,  and flashlight with
long-life batteries;                    Arms  or  weapons of any  kind
                                        unless approved by the Captain
No more than 10 lb of luggage,          or,  in the event of the death
including    prospecting   and          or  permanent  disablement  of
survival   equipment.   Excess          the   Captain  prior  to   the
baggage may be transported  at          conclusion of the  flight,  by
the discretion of the carrier,          another      duly      elected
at   a   fee  of  $1,000   per          authority.
additional ounce.
```

HOW TO CREATE A TWO-COLUMN FORMAT

You Enter . . .	*WordStar Comments and Important Notes*	
^ KH	Look good? Hide the block markers.	19
^ KN	Now turn off the column-move mode.	20
^ OR	To prepare for the next exercise, reset the right margin to its normal setting.	21
65 (Press RETURN.)	WordStar asks: RIGHT MARGIN COLUMN NUMBER (ESCAPE for cursor column)?	22
^ KD	Save the document and return to the no-file menu.	23

WHAT YOU JUST DID

You have used WordStar's column-move mode to paste up a page into left- and right-hand columns. If your document had been more than one page long when you typed it in a narrow column, you would have pasted up narrow-column pages 1 and 2 as two-column page 1, narrow-column pages 3 and 4 as two-column page 2, narrow-column pages 5 and 6 as two-column page 3, and so on.

Follow these steps to create a two-column format:

1. Open a document file.
2. Reset the right margin for the column width you want, using ^ OR. If your printer can only print 80 characters on each line, remember that each column can only be about 35 characters wide.
3. If you plan to use a letter-quality printer, type the command .UJ OFF at the beginning of the document to eliminate microspace justification.
4. Type your document and edit and reformat it as necessary. You will be unable to do any further editing once you paste up the right-hand column.
5. Tell WordStar to use its column-move mode with the command ^ KN.
6. Mark the beginning of the right-hand column text using the beginning block marker command ^ KB.
7. Move the cursor to the last line of the text that will appear in the right-hand column. Place the cursor in the space to the right of the right- margin setting. For example, if the right margin is set at column 20, place the cursor in column 21.
8. Mark the end of the right-hand column text using the ending block marker command ^ KK.
9. Move the cursor back up to the beginning of the document with ^ QR.

10. Reset the right margin so that it can accommodate the right-hand column.

11. Place the cursor where you want the first line of the right column to appear.

12. Tell WordStar to paste up the right-hand column using the block-move command ^KV.

13. The right-hand column is now properly pasted up. Repeat the process if your document is more than one two-column page long.

14. Save and print the document.

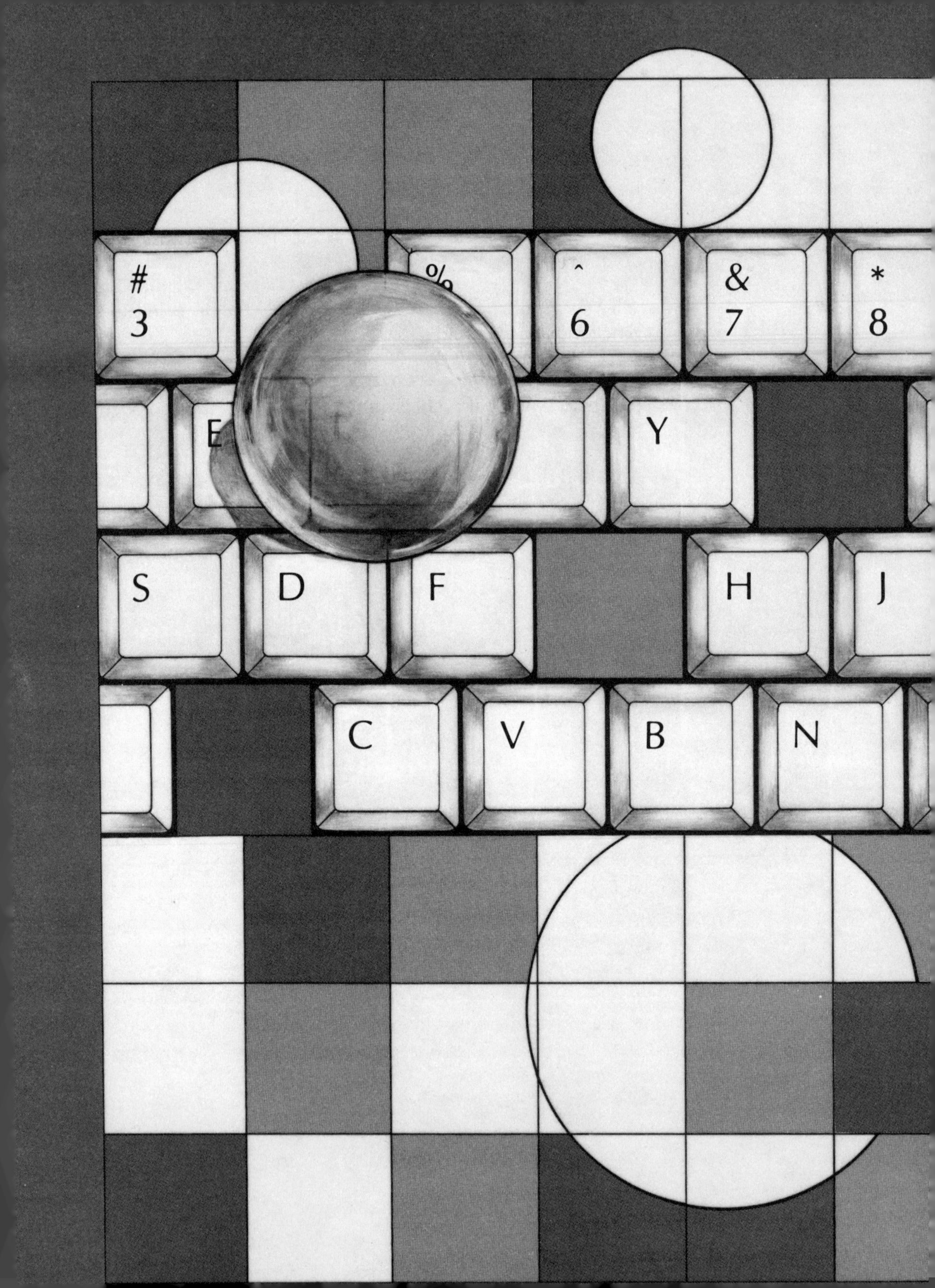
#
3
%
^
6
&
7
*
8
E
Y
S
D
F
H
J
C
V
B
N

eleven
Outline Formats

WHAT IS AN OUTLINE FORMAT?

An outline format is one in which main subject headings are typed flush with the left margin and successive subheadings are indented.

WHEN TO USE AN OUTLINE FORMAT

Many companies provide an outline to the people attending a corporate meeting, so that each person understands the purpose and scope of the meeting. Writers develop an outline of a proposed book, which is then modified and expanded as the book idea is discussed with an editor or coauthor. Some legal documents use an outline format, with different sections of text indented to indicate that they refer to preceding main subject headings.

WHAT YOU WILL DO

You can use a special WordStar command, ^OG, to reset the left margin temporarily to any one of the tabs currently set in the screen ruler line. Once you press RETURN to complete a paragraph, the left margin automatically resets itself to the standard left margin setting.

The command ^OG has one drawback, however. WordStar does not remember the temporary tab settings, so you have to reset the left margin to the indented setting before editing any indented section of text. To overcome this problem we have developed another way to create outline formats that we will explain once you have mastered the first ^OG method.

In this exercise, you will type an outline-format itinerary, using the command ^OG to indent different sections of text as you enter them. Then you will open a new file and will type a contract with a flush-left margin for all sections of text. You will be able to edit freely, because you will not yet have indented the subheadings. Once you are sure your contract is correct, you can use the ^ OG command together with WordStar's paragraph reformat command, ^ B, to indent your subheadings correctly.

HOW TO CREATE AN OUTLINE FORMAT

WordStar Comments and Important Notes	*You Enter . . .*
1 When the no-file menu appears on the screen, tell WordStar you want to create or edit a document.	D
2 WordStar asks: NAME OF FILE TO EDIT? WordStar flashes NEW FILE, then transports you to the edit mode.	AD.CPY (Press RETURN.)
3 When the main menu appears on the screen, you want to begin your outline by typing a title. Type the title at the left margin. When you have finished, instead of pressing RETURN, use the command ^ OC to tell WordStar to center the title. After WordStar has centered the title, press RETURN.	ITINERARY ^ OC (Press RETURN.)
4 Use the RETURN key to move the cursor down to line four. Now type your first heading flush with the left margin.	TRANSPORTATION TO THE SPACEPORT: (Press RETURN.)

HOW TO CREATE AN OUTLINE FORMAT

You Enter . . .	*WordStar Comments and Important Notes*	
(Press RETURN.)	Use the RETURN to key to space down so that there is one blank line between this heading and the first line of text.	5
^OG	Enter the command ^OG to reset the left margin temporarily to the first tab setting. On some video displays, the ruler line will brighten from the left margin to the first tab to let you know that the left margin has been temporarily reset. On other displays the ruler line may fade or appear in reverse video from the left margin to the first tab. WordStar uses whatever video capabilities are available to visually highlight a temporary margin setting. If your video display is incapable of highlighting sections of the screen, you will only know that the margin has been reset when the text begins in the correct column position.	6
(Enter text.)	Enter the first paragraph overleaf. Do not worry about indenting the lines of text—WordStar will automatically indent them for you as you go along.	7

```
                         ITINERARY
TRANSPORTATION TO THE SPACEPORT:

    Chauffeured air cars will transport all passengers from their
    domiciles,  provided  they are within 1,000 nautical miles of
    the spaceport.
```

WordStar Comments and Important Notes	*You Enter . . .*
8 Use the RETURN key to space down so that there is a blank line between the last line of that paragraph and the next one you will type.	(Press RETURN.)
9 This paragraph will be indented to the second tab, so enter the command ^ OG twice. The ruler line may change in some way to indicate the temporary setting (see instruction 6).	^ OG ^ OG
10 Type the rest of the text on the next page. Notice that the command ^ OG appears one or two times at the beginning of some of the text paragraphs. Before typing each paragraph, enter the command ^ OG as many times as indicated. The ruler line may change intensity as you enter the command to let you know where the left margin is temporarily set for that paragraph.	(Enter text.)

```
                         ITINERARY

TRANSPORTATION TO THE SPACEPORT:

     Chauffeured air cars will transport all passengers from their
     domiciles,  provided  they are within 1,000 nautical miles of
     the spaceport.

(^OG^OG)WHILE   IN   TRANSIT,   ENJOY   THE   LUXURY   OF   PERSONALIZED
SERVICE  FROM  OUR CHARMING FLIGHT ATTENDANTS.  NO-HOST  BAR  AND
GRILL AVAILABLE ON BOARD.

STOP-OVERS AND FLY-BYS:

(^OG)A  1-week stop-over on Mars is scheduled to allow passengers
to  visit  the ruined canals and other natural  wonders  of  that
planet. Depending on orbital peculiarities, stop-overs or fly-bys
are  also  scheduled for Jupiter and Uranus.  If  passengers  are
unable   to   spend  time  on  these   planets,   the   in-flight
entertainment   director  will  provide  information  about   the
possiblities of visiting and exploring any as-yet-unknown planets
discovered en route.

(^OG^OG)BE  ONE  OF THE FIRST HUMAN BEINGS TO ACTUALLY  ROAM  THE
ROMANTIC  AND MYSTERIOUS MARTIAN RUINS.  TAKE THE OPPORTUNITY  TO
DISCOVER,  EXPLORE,  AND  CLAIM  WHOLE  CONTINENTS  NEVER  BEFORE
VISITED BY MAN.

IN-FLIGHT ENTERTAINMENT:

(^OG)A variety of pleasure centers have been established on board
the   USS  Orwell  to  ensure  that  passengers  mingle,  enjoy
themselves,  and  stay  somewhat rational on this long voyage  of
discovery.

(^OG^OG)TRY YOUR HAND AT FREE-FALL SHUFFLEBOARD. GET THE BEST TAN
OF  YOUR LIFE IN OUR SOLAR VILLAGES.  JOIN THE CAPTAIN'S POOL  TO
ESTIMATE THE EFFECTS OF SPACE TRAVEL ON THE NEXT GENERATION. TAKE
TIME TO READ THE WORLD'S GREATEST LITERATURE.

DESTINATION:

(^OG)We  don't  yet know where the USS Orwell is  going,  and  we
don't  yet know when it will arrive.  But we do know that  you'll
have the time of the rest of your life just getting there!
```

ITINERARY

TRANSPORTATION TO THE SPACEPORT:

Chauffeured air cars will transport all passengers from their domiciles, provided they are within 1,000 nautical miles of the spaceport.

WHILE IN TRANSIT, ENJOY THE LUXURY OF PERSONALIZED SERVICE FROM OUR CHARMING FLIGHT ATTENDANTS. NO-HOST BAR AND GRILL AVAILABLE ON BOARD.

STOP-OVERS AND FLY-BYS:

A 1-week stop-over on Mars is scheduled to allow passengers to visit the ruined canals and other natural wonders of that planet. Depending on orbital peculiarities, stop-overs or fly-bys are also scheduled for Jupiter and Uranus. If passengers are unable to spend time on these planets, the in-flight entertainment director will provide information about the possiblities of visiting and exploring any as-yet-unknown planets discovered en route.

BE ONE OF THE FIRST HUMAN BEINGS TO ACTUALLY ROAM THE ROMANTIC AND MYSTERIOUS MARTIAN RUINS. TAKE THE OPPORTUNITY TO DISCOVER, EXPLORE, AND CLAIM WHOLE CONTINENTS NEVER BEFORE VISITED BY MAN.

IN-FLIGHT ENTERTAINMENT:

A variety of pleasure centers have been established on board the USS Orwell to ensure that passengers mingle, enjoy themselves, and stay somewhat rational on this long voyage of discovery.

TRY YOUR HAND AT FREE-FALL SHUFFLEBOARD. GET THE BEST TAN OF YOUR LIFE IN OUR SOLAR VILLAGES. JOIN THE CAPTAIN'S POOL TO ESTIMATE THE EFFECTS OF SPACE TRAVEL ON THE NEXT GENERATION. TAKE TIME TO READ THE WORLD'S GREATEST LITERATURE.

DESTINATION:

We don't yet know where the USS Orwell is going, and we don't yet know when it will arrive. But we do know that you'll have the time of the rest of your life just getting there!

HOW TO CREATE AN OUTLINE FORMAT

You Enter . . .	*WordStar Comments and Important Notes*	
(Compare texts.)	If you entered the document correctly, it should look like the one on the facing page.	11
(Correct any errors.)	If you made any typographical errors that have to be corrected, remember that WordStar has forgotten that you set special temporary tabs. You will have to move to the place where you made the error, correct it, position the cursor on the first character of the paragraph, enter the appropriate number of ^ OG commands, and then use WordStar's reformat command, ^ B. If you forget to reset the temporary left margin before using ^ B, WordStar will reformat the paragraph to your normal left margin setting.	12
^ KD	Now tell WordStar to save this outline so you can return to the no-file menu to make another selection.	13

WHAT YOU JUST DID

In this part of the exercise, you have practiced using WordStar's temporary, left-margin reset command while entering text, to create an immediate outline format.

The advantage of creating a special format while entering text is that you see immediately how the finished document will look. The disadvantage of formatting while entering text is that later editing requires a little more attention on your part. After inserting or deleting text, you must remember to reset the indented left margin before you reformat.

For another way to create an outline format, read on.

HOW TO CREATE AN OUTLINE FORMAT THAT IS EASIER TO EDIT

WordStar Comments and Important Notes	***You Enter . . .***
1 When the no-file menu appears on your screen, tell WordStar you want to create or edit a document.	D
2 WordStar asks: NAME OF FILE TO EDIT? WordStar flashes the comment NEW FILE, then transports you to the edit mode.	CONTRACT (Press RETURN.)
3 Enter the document you see on the next page. After typing each line of the title, remember to use the command ^OC to center the line before you press RETURN.	(Enter text.)
4 Proofread your document and correct any errors. Reformat corrected paragraphs as you go along, using the command ^B.	(Correct any errors.)

```
                    ESCAPE PLEASURE CRUISES
                      PASSENGER CONTRACT

The  undersigned  agrees that ESCAPE has been assigned  power  of
attorney  to administer his/her estate.  The powers  invested  in
ESCAPE include, but are not limited to:

Absolute  governmental,  military,  and  economic control of  all
discoveries  made  by  the undersigned while  in  transit  to  an
unknown  destination including,  but not limited to,  discoveries
that are animal, vegetable, mineral, or indescribable in nature.

In  addition,  the  undersigned waives the  following  litigation
rights while in transit to an unknown destination:

ESCAPE  may not be sued by the undersigned or his/her assigns  in
the event of the physical,  emotional,  or mental collapse of the
undersigned.

ESCAPE  may not be sued by the undersigned or his/her assigns  in
the   event  that  the  undersigned  never  actually  reaches   a
destination of any description.

-----------------------------------   ------------------------
        Signature                               Date
```

You Enter . . .	WordStar Comments and Important Notes	
^OH	Before creating the outline format, turn OFF hyphen-help so you will not have to stop and hyphenate words while reformatting your contract.	**5**
(Use cursor-movement commands as necessary.)	Now move the cursor to the letter *A* in the word *Absolute,* the first word in the second paragraph.	**6**

HOW TO CREATE AN OUTLINE FORMAT THAT IS EASIER TO EDIT

	WordStar Comments and Important Notes	***You Enter . . .***
7	Temporarily reset the left margin to the first tab stop.	^ OG
8	Reformat this paragraph.	^ B
9	Move the cursor to the letter *I* in the word *In* at the beginning of the third paragraph.	(Use cursor-movement commands as necessary.)
10	Temporarily reset the left margin to the first tab stop.	^ OG
11	Reformat this paragraph to the new margin setting.	^ B
12	Move the cursor to the letter *E* in the word *ESCAPE,* the first word in the fourth paragraph.	(Use cursor-movement commands as necessary.)
13	Reset the left margin to the second tab stop.	^ OG ^ OG
14	Reformat this paragraph.	^ B

HOW TO CREATE AN OUTLINE FORMAT THAT IS EASIER TO EDIT

You Enter . . .	*WordStar Comments and Important Notes*	
(Use cursor-movement commands as necessary.)	Move the cursor to the letter *E* in the word *ESCAPE* at the beginning of the last paragraph.	**15**
^ OG ^ OG	Temporarily reset the left margin to the second tab stop.	**16**
^ B	Reformat this paragraph.	**17**
(Compare contracts.)	That's it! Your contract should look like the one on the next page.	**18**
^ KD	If everything looks good, save the document.	**19**

```
                    ESCAPE PLEASURE CRUISES
                      PASSENGER CONTRACT

The  undersigned  agrees that ESCAPE has been assigned  power  of
attorney  to administer his/her estate.  The powers  invested  in
ESCAPE include, but are not limited to:

     Absolute governmental, military, and economic control of all
     discoveries  made by the undersigned while in transit to  an
     unknown   destination   including,   but   not   limited   to,
     discoveries   that   are   animal,    vegetable,    mineral,    or
     indescribable in nature.

     In addition, the undersigned waives the following litigation
     rights while in transit to an unknown destination:

          ESCAPE  may not be sued by the undersigned  or  his/her
          assigns  in the event of the  physical,  emotional,  or
          mental collapse of the undersigned.

          ESCAPE  may  not be sued by the undersigned or  his/her
          assigns  in  the  event  that  the  undersigned   never
          actually reaches a destination of any description.

-----------------------------------    ------------------------
             Signature                          Date
```

WHAT YOU JUST DID

You have just avoided the problem of WordStar forgetting your temporary margin settings when you try to edit an outline. You have entered your entire document using WordStar's standard margin settings and edited your text. You were then able to go back through the document and selectively reset the margins and reformat certain sections of text.

Three important things to remember when using the command ^OG:

1. The command ^OG resets the left margin to a specified tab setting. You specify which tab by entering the command ^OG as many times as necessary to move the left margin to the appropriate tab stop. For example, to set the left margin at the third tab stop, you must enter the command ^OG^OG^OG.

2. This command only resets the left margin temporarily. The left margin will return to the standard ruler-line setting once you press RETURN after typing a paragraph. If you are using ^ B to reformat a paragraph with a temporary margin setting, the left margin will return to the standard ruler line setting when WordStar encounters a carriage return.

3. WordStar does not remember your temporary margin settings; you have to remember them. If you later edit an indented paragraph, you will have to reset the temporary margin using the command ^ OG, then enter the ^ B reformatting command.

#
3
^
6
&
7
*
8
Y
S
D
F
H
J
C
V
B
N

twelve

Tabs and Decimal Tabs

WHAT ARE TABS AND DECIMAL TABS?

When you are using a typewriter, you can jump from one point to another on the same line by setting a marker called a tab at each position. Your typewriter remembers these points, and will move from position to position each time you press a key labeled TAB. WordStar lets you set, reset, and use tabs in a similar fashion.

Because WordStar is so much smarter than a typewriter, it can also remember where decimal points should appear in columns of numbers. With WordStar, you can set decimal tabs so you can jump from one column to another and land in the right place to enter a perfectly aligned decimal point.

When you use a decimal tab, you enter numbers just as you would on a calculator. Just jump to the tab and begin typing the number. Until you type a decimal point, WordStar will push all numbers to the left of the tab position. Once you enter a decimal point, WordStar will begin pushing numbers to the right of the decimal point. So, whether or not you are actually typing decimal points, WordStar's decimal tabs will make sure your numbers are always properly aligned.

The WordStar ruler line appears at the top of the screen whenever you enter the edit mode. Besides noting left and right margin settings, it is used to display all tab settings. A regular tab is indicated by a ! in the ruler line. A decimal tab is indicated by a # in the ruler line.

WHEN TO USE TABS AND DECIMAL TABS

Use WordStar's regular tabs the same way you would use tabs on a typewriter. Use WordStar's decimal tab feature whenever you have to line up columns of numbers—even if they do not include decimal points. When you use decimal tabs, you can stop worrying about counting the number of characters in each number so you can line them all up properly.

WHAT YOU WILL DO

Once you have opened a new file, you will clear all tab settings. Then you will set one regular tab and one decimal tab so you can enter words and numbers. Finally, you will type a sample budget, using either your terminal's TAB key or WordStar's ^I key to jump from tab to tab.

HOW TO USE TABS AND DECIMAL TABS

WordStar Comments and Important Notes	*You Enter . . .*
1 When the no-file menu appears on the screen, tell WordStar you want to create a document.	D
2 WordStar asks: NAME OF FILE TO EDIT? WordStar flashes NEW FILE, then transports you to the edit mode.	BUDGET (Press RETURN.)
3 The first thing you must do is clear all existing tab settings, which are marked by exclamation points in the ruler line.	^ON

HOW TO USE TABS AND DECIMAL TABS

You Enter . . .	*WordStar Comments and Important Notes*	
A (Press RETURN.)	WordStar asks: CLEAR TAB AT COL (ESCAPE for cursor col; A for all)? Notice that all exclamation points have disappeared from the ruler line, letting you know that all tabs have been cleared.	**4**
^ OI	Now tell WordStar you want to set your first tab.	**5**
6 (Press RETURN.)	WordStar asks: For decimal tab stop enter "#" and decimal point column SET TAB AT COLUMN (ESCAPE for cursor column)? Notice that an exclamation point has appeared in column 6 of your ruler line. That marks your first tab setting.	**6**
^ OI	Now tell WordStar you want to set another tab.	**7**
# 59 (Press RETURN.)	WordStar asks: For decimal tab stop enter "#" and decimal point column SET TAB AT COLUMN (ESCAPE for cursor column)? Now a # has appeared at column 59 of your ruler line, letting you know that you have set a decimal tab.	**8**

HOW TO USE TABS AND DECIMAL TABS

WordStar Comments and Important Notes	*You Enter . . .*
9 Now you are ready to use these tabs. Enter the income budget you see below. Wherever you see the command ^ I, enter that command to move to the next tab stop, then continue typing the text or numbers that follow. When you type numbers, be sure to type them just as you read them, from left to right. Don't worry about lining them up—WordStar will take care of that for you.	(Enter projected income budget.)

```
                    ADVERTISING INCOME AND EXPENSE

PROJECTED INCOME

(^I)Product endorsements:

(^I)Dolls(^I)1,000,000.00
(^I)Athletic clothing(^I)10,000,000.00
(^I)Sports equipment(^I)30,000,000.00
(^I)Health foods(^I)15,000,000.00
(^I)Jewelry(^I)42,000,000.00

(^I)Advertising space on USS Orwell:

(^I)10,000 sq ft x 500,000/sq ft(^I)5,000,000,000.00

Total Income (^I)5,113,000,000.00
```

```
                    ADVERTISING INCOME AND EXPENSE

PROJECTED INCOME
     Product endorsements:

     Dolls                                          1,000,000.00
     Athletic clothing                             10,000,000.00
     Sports equipment                              30,000,000.00
     Health foods                                  15,000,000.00
     Jewelry                                       42,000,000.00

     Advertising space on USS Orwell:

     10,000 sq ft x 500,000/sq ft               5,000,000,000.00

Total Income                                    5,113,000,000.00
```

You Enter . . .	***WordStar Comments and Important Notes***	
(Compare budgets.)	If you did everything properly, your budget should look like the one above.	**10**
(Correct errors.)	If your budget does not look like this, you may have been confused by the decimal tab and accidentally spaced forward or backward before you began typing a number. When you do that, WordStar thinks you do not really want to use the decimal tab. If decimal tabs did not seem to work for you, first move the cursor back to the incorrect line and turn INSERT OFF using ^V if necessary. Then tab over to the decimal tab with ^I and immediately begin typing the correct number.	**11**

HOW TO USE TABS AND DECIMAL TABS

WordStar Comments and Important Notes	***You Enter . . .***
12 Once you have completed your corrections, save this budget. Use the save command that saves the document then transports you directly to the operating system. As you may have discovered, WordStar remembers the ruler line margin and tab settings you have changed and will retain the same ruler line for each succeeding document unless you change it or exit WordStar to automatically return the ruler line to the standard settings. To prepare for the next exercise, we have asked you to exit WordStar. CP/M or IBM PC-DOS responds: B>	^ KX
13 Return to WordStar for the next exercise. Include the drive identifier A: with the command to run WordStar, since WordStar is stored on the disk in drive A. You will use the budget you just created to develop a ruler line that can be saved with your document, so you do not have to reset margins and tabs every time you want to edit it.	A:WS (Press RETURN.)

WHAT YOU JUST DID

You have just created some tabular material using your own tab and decimal tab settings. Here once again are the steps to follow:

1. Clear all tab settings by using the command ^ON followed by A.
2. Set regular tabs by using the command ^OI followed by the column number in which you want to set the tab.
3. Set decimal tabs by using the command ^OI followed by # (to tell WordStar you want to set a decimal tab) and the column number in which the decimal tab should appear.

#
3
%
^
6
&
7
*
8
E
Y
S
D
F
H
J
C
V
B
N

thirteen
Stored Ruler Lines

WHAT IS A STORED RULER LINE?

Whenever you enter WordStar's edit mode, WordStar displays a line of dashes across the top of your video screen. This is WordStar's built-in ruler line, which indicates your current margin and tab settings. The letters L and R mark the positions of the left and right margins. A ! on the line marks a regular tab setting, and a # marks a decimal tab setting. Whatever you type on the screen will be formatted using those settings.

You may change these settings each time you write or edit something, or you may create a ruler line that can be stored with a document. The stored ruler line can be used to reset margins and tabs automatically in the appropriate places each time you work on your document.

WHEN TO USE STORED RULER LINES

In the last few exercises, you learned how to change margins and tabs, and watched the ruler line display these changes. If you regularly use an unusual format, however, it is much more efficient to store the format with the document, so that WordStar can automatically match its ruler line to your format, rather than having to change the margins and tabs yourself each time. If you often update a columnar report with lots of tabs, you can save time by creating a ruler line that can be stored with the document.

WHAT YOU WILL DO

First you will open a new file, and create and implement a ruler line that includes the tabs you need for the budget you created in the last exercise. Then you will read in a copy of your budget and add a few more numbers.

To get a better idea of how ruler lines save time, you will save the file and exit to CP/M which automatically resets the ruler line back to the WordStar standard format. Then you will reenter WordStar, recall the budget, and use the stored ruler line to modify WordStar's built-in ruler line.

HOW TO CREATE AND USE A RULER LINE

WordStar Comments and Important Notes	*You Enter . . .*
1 When the no-file menu appears on the screen, tell WordStar you want to create or edit a document.	D
2 WordStar asks: NAME OF FILE TO EDIT? WordStar flashes NEW FILE and transports you to the edit mode.	NEWBUDGE (Press RETURN.)
3 When the edit-mode main menu appears on the screen, tell WordStar you are typing something that should appear on the screen, but not be printed as part of the document. Whenever WordStar encounters two periods in columns 1 and 2, it knows it should not print whatever text follows. To create a	.. ^ P (Press RETURN.)

HOW TO CREATE AND USE A RULER LINE

You Enter . . .	*WordStar Comments and Important Notes*	
	ruler line that will not print as part of the document, position the cursor at the left margin and type in .. for no print and ^ P RETURN to indicate that the next line should be treated as part of the previous non-printing line. In other words, ^ P RETURN tells WordStar to print the next line over the previous line. As soon as you press RETURN, WordStar acknowledges that it will not print the ruler line by displaying a hyphen in the right margin. ^ P will not appear on your screen; you will see .. on the left and - on the right. You are now ready to type a ruler line similar to the one that WordStar displays at the top of the screen. A line of dashes starting at the left margin and ending at the right margin indicates line length. You may insert ! or # anywhere on this line to indicate where tabs and decimal tabs should be set. As you may recall, the budget in the last exercise had a line length of 65 columns, a regular tab set at column 6, and a decimal tab set at column 59. Duplicate this ruler line.	
- - - - -	The cursor should be positioned in column 1 of the blank line that follows the two periods. Begin by typing five dashes.	4

HOW TO CREATE AND USE A RULER LINE

WordStar Comments and Important Notes		*You Enter . . .*
5	The top status line should indicate that the cursor is now positioned at column 6. Set your first tab here.	!
6	Continue entering dashes from column 7 through column 58. Stop when the status line indicates you have reached column 59.	- (From COL 7 through COL 58.)
7	Set a decimal tab in column 59.	#
8	Continue typing dashes from column 60 through column 65 to complete your ruler line.	- (From COL 60 through COL 65. Press RETURN.)
9	You have completed your budget ruler line. This is what it should look like:	(Compare ruler lines.)

```
                                                                                  -
..
-----!----------------------------------------------------#-----                  <
```

HOW TO CREATE AND USE A RULER LINE

You Enter . . .	*WordStar Comments and Important Notes*	
(Use cursor-movement commands as necessary.)	Now what? First make sure the cursor is positioned in column 1 of the blank line below the ruler line you just created.	**10**
^ KR	Then tell WordStar you want it to read in a copy of a file.	**11**
BUDGET (Press RETURN.)	WordStar asks: NAME OF FILE TO EDIT? Your file called BUDGET has appeared on the screen. Notice that, so far, your new ruler line has not had any effect on WordStar's built-in ruler line. You have to tell WordStar you want to implement it.	**12**
(Use cursor-movement commands as necessary.)	Move the cursor until it sits anywhere on your ruler line.	**13**
^ OF	Tell WordStar to adjust its ruler line to match yours. Notice that WordStar's ruler line has magically reset itself to follow your settings.	**14**

HOW TO CREATE AND USE A RULER LINE

WordStar Comments and Important Notes	*You Enter . . .*
15 Now you are ready to add numbers to to your budget, using your preset tabs. Move the cursor to the end of the current budget, and enter your expenses using WordStar's tab command ^I to skip from tab to tab as indicated in the text at the top of the next page.	(Enter expenses.)
16 If you did everything correctly, your new budget looks like the one at the bottom of the next page.	(Compare budgets.)
17 How do you use your ruler line next time you want to edit your budget? Pretend you have finished working for the day. Save this document and exit WordStar to DOS.	^KX
18 Now go back to WordStar. To save keystrokes and time, call up both WordStar from the disk in drive A and the document you want to edit by typing A:WS and the file name on the same line. You should have been transported immediately to the edit mode, with your NEWBUDGE file, complete with ruler line, on the screen. Notice that WordStar has reverted to its standard ruler line.	A:WS NEWBUDGE (Press RETURN.)

```
EXPENSES

(^I)Membership flyers(^I)1,550.25
(^I)Super Bowl 30-second spot(^I)615,328.57
(^I)Blimp rental for Super Bowl(^I)25,327.95
(^I)Bumper stickers(^I)532.50

Total Expenses (^I)642,739.27

ADVERTISING REVENUE PROFIT (^I)5,112,357,260.73
```

```
                    ADVERTISING INCOME AND EXPENSE

PROJECTED INCOME

     Product endorsements:

     Dolls                                            1,000,000.00
     Athletic clothing                               10,000,000.00
     Sports equipment                                30,000,000.00
     Health foods                                    15,000,000.00
     Jewelry                                         42,000,000.00

     Advertising space on USS Orwell:

     10,000 sq ft x 500,000/sq ft                 5,000,000,000.00

Total Income                                      5,113,000,000.00

EXPENSES

     Membership flyers                                    1,550.25
     Super Bowl 30-second spot                          615,328.57
     Blimp rental for Super Bowl                         25,327.95
     Bumper stickers                                        532.50

Total Expenses                                          642,739.27

ADVERTISING REVENUE PROFIT                        5,112,357,260.73
```

HOW TO CREATE AND USE A RULER LINE

WordStar Comments and Important Notes	*You Enter . . .*
19 To use the ruler line you created, start by positioning the cursor anywhere on the ruler line stored with the file.	(Use cursor-movement commands as necessary.)
20 Tell WordStar you want it to match this ruler line.	^ OF
21 Did WordStar's built-in ruler line change to match yours? Great! Now you are ready to begin typing again.	(Compare ruler lines.)
22 We do not have anything to add to this file, so why not abandon it? When you use the abandon-file command, the original file is retained on the disk but the version you see on your screen, which you may have modified, is discarded. WordStar will check to make sure you really want to abandon the file before actually throwing it away.	^ KQ

WHAT YOU JUST DID

You have just learned how to create and store a ruler line with a document so you do not have to figure out where to set margins and tabs every time you want to edit the document. Store a ruler line with every document formatted with special margins or tabs that you modify regularly or expect to have to edit.

This is how to create a ruler line:

1. Position the cursor in column 1 of the first blank line in your new file. Enter the command .. ^ P and press RETURN.
2. Begin typing dashes, starting in the column that marks your left margin.
3. As you type the line of dashes, insert a ! wherever you want to set a regular tab and a # wherever you want to set a decimal tab.
4. Continue typing dashes until the cursor reaches the column that marks your right margin. Then just press RETURN.
5. Save this ruler line as part of your document.
6. Whenever you want to use the ruler line, place the cursor anywhere on it and enter the command ^ OF. WordStar's built-in ruler line will change to match the one you created and stored.

#
3
%
^
6
&
7
*
8
E
Y
S
D
F
H
J
C
V
B
N

fourteen

Multiple Stored Ruler Lines

WHEN TO USE MULTIPLE STORED RULER LINES

Sometimes creating one ruler line for a document is not enough. If you frequently change margins to type quotations, if you write scripts with audio instructions formatted one way and video instructions another, or if you type reports that include columnar tables, you know how tedious it is to change margins and tabs back and forth so you can type different parts of the same document.

With WordStar, you can create several special ruler lines, each stored in its own file. Whenever you need a particular line, you read it into your document, tell WordStar to change its built-in ruler line to match, and go right on typing.

WHAT YOU WILL DO

First you will open a new file, create a ruler line, and save it. You will do the same for a second ruler line. Then you will open a third new file, read in your first ruler line, implement it, and type a paragraph within its margins. You will read in your second ruler line, implement it, and type another paragraph. This sequence will be repeated so you can practice switching back and forth between ruler lines.

HOW TO CREATE AND USE MULTIPLE STORED RULER LINES

	WordStar Comments and Important Notes	***You Enter . . .***
1	When the no-file menu appears on the screen, tell WordStar you want to create or edit a document.	D
2	WordStar asks: NAME OF FILE TO EDIT? WordStar flashes NEW FILE, then transports you to the edit mode. You are going to create a ruler line for video script instructions.	R1 (Press RETURN.)
3	Position the cursor in column 1 of the first line and tell WordStar you want to create a non-printing line.	.. ^ P (Press RETURN.)
4	Position the cursor in column 6. Watch the status line to know when you reach the right place.	(Press space bar as necessary.)
5	Enter dashes from column 6 through column 56 to set a line length of 50 characters. (The status line will read COL 57 when you are finished.)	- (From COL 6 through COL 56. Press RETURN.)
6	This is your first ruler line. Save it.	^ KD

HOW TO CREATE AND USE MULTIPLE STORED RULER LINES

You Enter . . .	*WordStar Comments and Important Notes*	
D	When the no-file menu reappears on the screen, tell WordStar you want to create or edit a document.	**7**
R2 (Press RETURN.)	WordStar asks: NAME OF FILE TO EDIT? WordStar flashes NEW FILE, then transports you to the edit mode. This time you will create a ruler line for the audio portions of your script.	**8**
.. ^ P (Press RETURN.)	Position the cursor in column 1 of the first line and tell WordStar you want to create a non-printing line. If when you print your document the ruler lines end up being printed too, you probably have not set up your ruler lines properly. Make sure that the periods appear in columns 1 and 2, followed immediately by a ^ P and a RETURN.	**9**
(Use cursor-movement commands as necessary.)	Position the cursor in column 16. Watch the status line to know when you reach the right place.	**10**
- (From COL 16 through COL 46. Press RETURN.)	Enter dashes from column 16 through column 46 to set a line length of 30 characters. (The status line will read COL 47 when you are finished.)	**11**

HOW TO CREATE AND USE MULTIPLE STORED RULER LINES

WordStar Comments and Important Notes	***You Enter . . .***
12 This is your second ruler line. Save it.	^ KD
13 When the no-file menu reappears on the screen, tell WordStar you want to create or edit a document.	D
14 WordStar asks: NAME OF FILE TO EDIT? WordStar flashes NEW FILE then transports you to the edit mode.	SCRIPT (Press RETURN.)
15 Tell WordStar you want to read in a file.	^ KR
16 WordStar asks: NAME OF FILE TO READ?	R1 (Press RETURN.)
17 When your first ruler line appears on the screen, move the cursor until it sits anywhere on the line. Then tell WordStar you want to implement the ruler line.	^ OF
18 Enter the text you see on the next page, remembering to center the title with ^ OC before you press RETURN.	(Enter text.)

```
..
    --------------------------------------------------------
                 1984 SUPER BOWL ADVERTISEMENT

    Lights   up.  Retired  football  player  sits   in
    overstuffed  chair  in den,  staring  pensively  at
    crackling fire.  Camera pans around den to focus on
    different  awards and pennants player has collected
    during his career. Back to player for voice-over.
```

You Enter . . .	WordStar Comments and Important Notes	
^ KR	Press RETURN twice, then tell WordStar you want to read in another file.	19
R2 (Press RETURN.)	WordStar asks: NAME OF FILE TO READ?	20
^ OF	Once the new ruler line appears, position the cursor anywhere on the line. Then tell WordStar you want to change your margins to match the new ruler line.	21
(Enter text.)	After WordStar's built-in ruler line has changed to match yours, enter the text you see on the next page, remembering to center the heading with ^ OC before you press RETURN.	22

```
..
                    --------------------------------
                               VOICE-OVER

                    Super Bowl Sunday.  What a drag
                    when  you're  not part  of  the
                    game. Where can a rich, retired
                    football   hero   find   a   new
                    challenge?
```

WordStar Comments and Important Notes	*You Enter . . .*
23 Press RETURN twice after finishing the paragraph. It is time to type some more video instructions, so tell WordStar you are ready to go back to the video ruler line.	^ KR
24 WordStar asks: NAME OF FILE TO READ?	R1 (Press RETURN.)
25 Position the cursor anywhere on the ruler line and implement its margin settings.	^ OF
26 Now enter the text on the next page.	(Enter text.)

```
..
      --------------------------------------------------------

      Player  sits up as mysterious,  helmeted face forms
      in  flames.  We hear the voice of the famous  Knute
      Rockne.
```

You Enter . . .	*WordStar Comments and Important Notes*	
^ KR	Now back to the audio ruler line.	**27**
R2 (Press RETURN.)	WordStar asks: NAME OF FILE TO READ?	**28**
^ OF	Position the cursor anywhere on the ruler line and implement it.	**29**
(Enter text.)	After WordStar's built-in ruler line has changed to match yours, enter the text on the next page, remembering to center the heading with ^ OC before you press RETURN.	**30**

```
..
          --------------------------------
                   KNUTE ROCKNE

          Hey,  remember  me?  I'm  the
          famous  Knute Rockne.  Why  not
          ESCAPE  like I  did?  Write  to
          this  address to learn how  you
          too   can    recapture     the
          excitement   of   a touchdown  by
          looking for that ultimate  goal
          somewhere in space.
```

WordStar Comments and Important Notes	*You Enter . . .*
31 Get the picture? Your finished advertisement script should look like the one on the facing page. When you print the script, it will look just like this, except that the dots and ruler lines will not appear as part of the document.	(Compare texts.)
32 Save this document.	^ KD

```
..
        ------------------------------------------------------------
                           1984 SUPERBOWL AD

        Lights   up.   Retired   football   player   sits    in
        overstuffed  chair   in den,  staring  pensively  at
        crackling fire.  Camera pans around den to focus on
        different  awards and pennants player has collected
        during his career. Back to player for voice-over.

..
                    ------------------------------------
                               VOICE-OVER

                    Super Bowl Sunday.  What a drag
                    when  you're  not  part  of  the
                    game. Where can a rich, retired
                    football    hero   find   a   new
                    challenge?
..
        ------------------------------------------------------------
        Player  sits up as mysterious,  helmeted face forms
        in  flames.  We hear the voice of the famous  Knute
        Rockne.

..
                    ------------------------------------
                              KNUTE ROCKNE

                    Hey,   remember  me?   I'm  the
                    famous  Knute Rockne.  Why  not
                    ESCAPE  like  I did?  Write  to
                    this  address to learn how  you
                    too     can     recapture    the
                    excitement  of a  touchdown  by
                    looking  for that ultimate goal
                    somewhere in space.
```

WHAT YOU JUST DID

Congratulations! Little by little you are learning how to use WordStar's built-in capabilities to save you time and energy. You have just created different ruler lines to match the different margin settings you needed within a document.

Follow these steps to create as many ruler lines as you need to match all the margin and tab settings you use regularly:

1. Create your ruler lines as described in the previous exercise, assigning each one a separate file name.
2. Whenever you need a stored ruler line, use ^KR to tell WordStar to read it into the file you are working on.
3. Position the cursor on the line and implement it with ^OF.

As you have seen, there is no limit to the number of different ruler lines you can use in the same document to avoid manually changing margins and tabs. In the next exercise, you will learn how to include other format information in the same file as the ruler line to really save your typing time.

#
3
%
^
6
&
7
*
8
E
Y
S
D
F
H
J
C
V
B
N

fifteen

Special Document Formats

WHAT IS A SPECIAL DOCUMENT FORMAT?

WordStar has built-in document formats that control the printed look of your documents by prescribing margin settings, tab settings, number of lines per page, and so on. Below are some of the standard formats that are built into WordStar:

Page length	66 lines	(8½ x 11—6 lines/in)
Page width	80 columns	(8½ x 11—10 characters/in)
Typed lines/ page	55 lines	(8½ x 11—single space)
Top margin	3 lines	(text starts on 4th line of page)
Bottom margin	8 lines	(text ends on 58th line of page)
Page offset	8 columns	(text starts at column 9)
Left margin	column 1	(really column 9)
Right margin	column 65	(really column 74)
Characters/line	65 characters	
Tab settings	every 5th column	
Page number	bottom center	

These standard settings produce a printed page that looks like this:

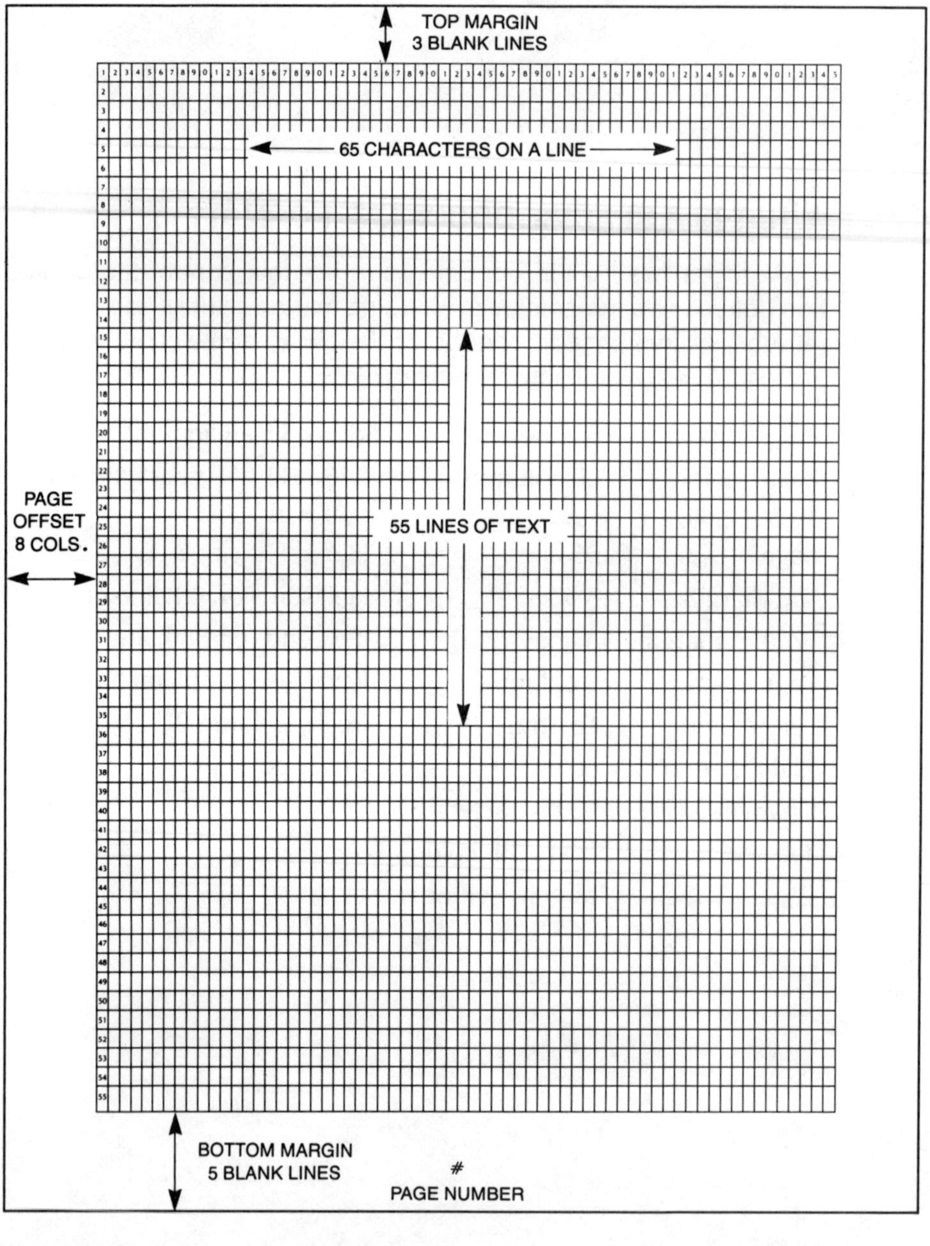

Figure 15.1: *Standard WordStar Page Format*

You can change any standard format setting. As you already know, you can change left and right margins (line length) and tab settings by creating a ruler line that duplicates the settings you want. You can also change page length, number of typed lines per page, page offset, and top and bottom margins by imbedding dot commands at the beginning of your document. A change to any standard setting creates a special document format. For example, the ruler lines you created in the previous exercise were actually special document formats.

WHEN TO USE SPECIAL DOCUMENT FORMATS

Most of us find that we are constantly changing one or two of WordStar's standard format settings because we always use a format that is not built into WordStar. Perhaps you type a lot of reports with columns of figures. Or maybe you prefer different margin and tab settings, a different page length, or offset pages.

Rather than having to enter these changes for each document, you can use WordStar features to create and store special formats that are inserted before you begin typing.

WHAT YOU WILL DO

First you will determine the format you want to produce. You need to know what size paper you will be using and to calculate what your margin settings should be. Then you will create a file to hold the commands that will produce the format you want. You will save this file and then use ^ KR to tell WordStar to read the format commands into the file of the document you want to create.

HOW TO CALCULATE SPECIAL FORMAT REQUIREMENTS

Practice creating special formats by running through the steps to produce a memo. Many companies use both standard 8½ x 11-in. business stationery and smaller-format company memo paper for short notes. To format these notes on company memo paper you have to reset some of WordStar's standard format characteristics so that the text prints properly on the smaller paper. Below is a sample memo paper sheet with the external dimensions marked, as well as the dimensions we want for the text that we are going to print.

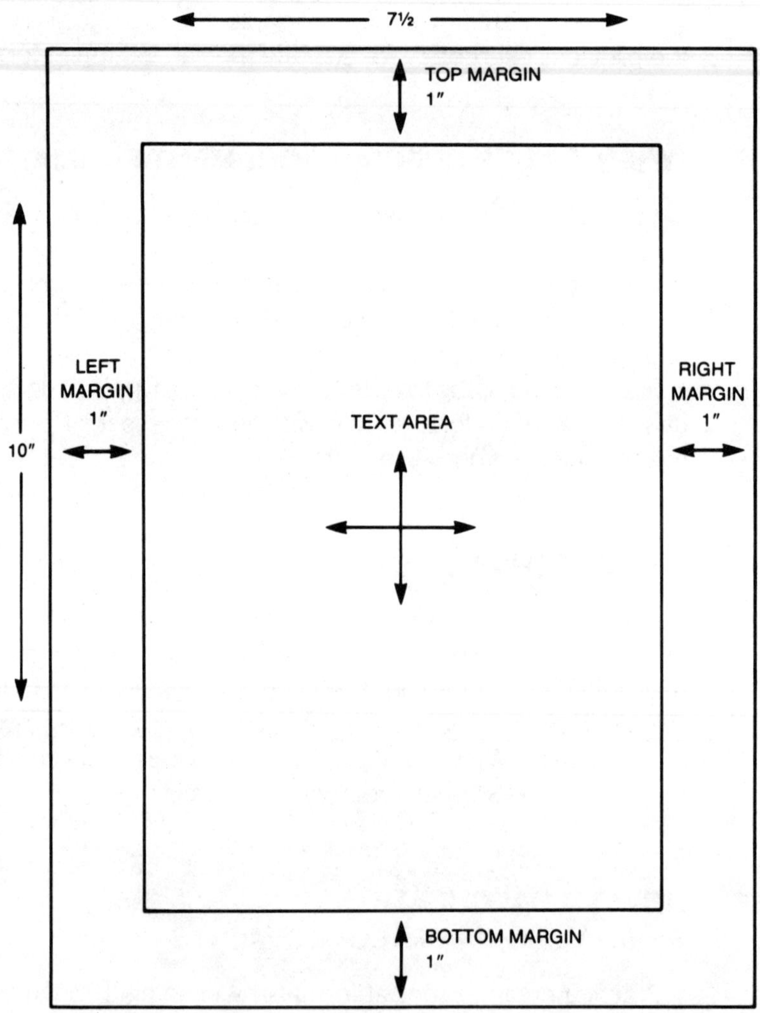

Figure 15.2: *Memo Format Requirements*

Once you have calculated the format requirements in terms of inches, you have to translate them into units of measure that WordStar can understand. WordStar thinks in terms of lines and columns, printing six lines to a vertical inch and ten columns, or characters, to a horizontal inch unless you tell it otherwise. You calculate the memo format for WordStar as follows:

Format	*Memo*	×	*Standard*	=	*WordStar Setting*
Page length	10	×	6 lines/in	=	60 lines
Page width	7½	×	10 col/in	=	75 columns
Top margin	1	×	6 lines/in	=	6 lines
Bottom margin	1	×	6 lines/in	=	6 lines
Page offset (left margin)	1	×	10 col/in	=	10 columns
Right margin	1	×	10 col/in	=	10 columns

Line length = page width – (page offset + right margin)

= 75 col – (10 col + 10 col) = 55 columns

From WordStar's point of view, this is what your memo paper format will look like:

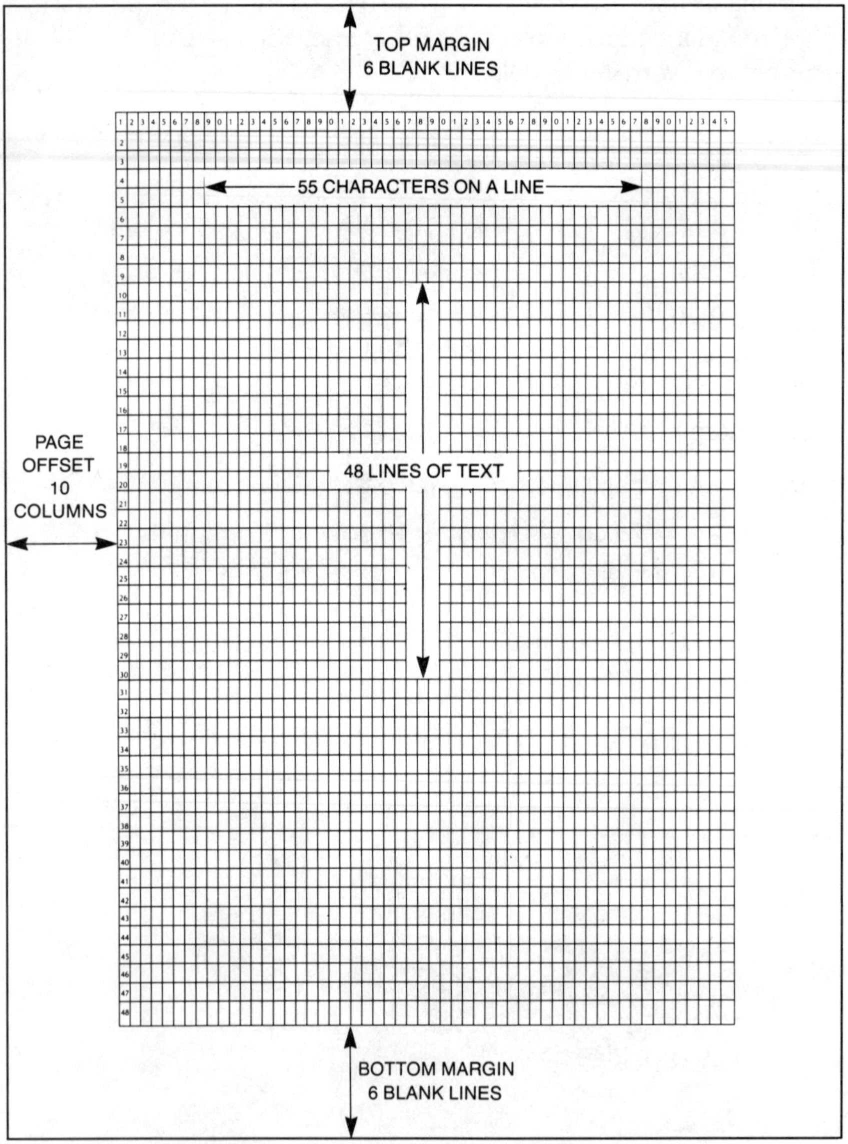

Figure 15.3: *WordStar Memo Format*

HOW TO CREATE AND USE A SPECIAL DOCUMENT FORMAT

You Enter . . .	*WordStar Comments and Important Notes*	
D	When the no-file menu is displayed on the screen, tell WordStar you want to create a new document.	1
MEMO.FMT (Press RETURN.)	WordStar asks: NAME OF FILE TO EDIT? WordStar flashes the comment NEW FILE, then transports you to the edit mode. You are now going to enter the format commands. Remember that they are dot commands, each beginning with a period that must appear in column 1, at the screen's left margin. There must be no spaces within the command, although you may put a space between the command and the format numbers you enter. Each command is completed by pressing RETURN, and each command must be typed on a line by itself.	2
.PL 60 (Press RETURN.)	First tell WordStar that the memo paper is only 60 lines long.	3
.MT 6 (Press RETURN.)	Now tell WordStar that the top margin consists of six blank lines.	4

HOW TO CREATE AND USE A SPECIAL DOCUMENT FORMAT

	WordStar Comments and Important Notes	*You Enter . . .*
5	Tell WordStar that the bottom margin also consists of six blank lines.	.MB 6 (Press RETURN.)
6	Tell WordStar that the page offset (left margin) is 10 columns wide.	.PO 10 (Press RETURN.)
7	Now tell WordStar that you do not want page numbers printed on the memo paper.	.OP (Press RETURN.)
8	Now you need to set the line length, and set a tab so you can easily type in the date and signature. To do this, you need to create a ruler line as you did in the last two exercises. Start by telling WordStar you want to create a non-printing line. When you enter the command correctly, a hyphen appears in the right-hand column of the command line. When you press RETURN, WordStar positions the cursor on the blank line just below the two periods.	.. ^ P (Press RETURN.)
9	Begin typing your ruler line. Enter a line of dashes from column 1 through column 26. Watch the status line so you know when you have reached column 27.	- (From COL 1 through COL 26.)

HOW TO CREATE AND USE A SPECIAL DOCUMENT FORMAT

You Enter . . .	*WordStar Comments and Important Notes*	
!	With the cursor positioned in column 27, enter an exclamation point to mark a tab setting for the date and signature block.	**10**
- (From COL 28 through COL 55.)	Now continue entering dashes from column 28 through column 55. (The status line will read COL 56 when you are finished.)	**11**
(Compare commands.)	You have completed your special format for memos. It should look like the one below.	**12**
^ KD	If everything looks correct, save this file.	**13**

```
.PL 60
.MT 6
.MB 6
.PO 10
.OP
..
--------------------------!---------------------------
```

HOW TO CREATE AND USE A SPECIAL DOCUMENT FORMAT

	WordStar Comments and Important Notes	***You Enter . . .***
14	When the no-file menu is displayed on the screen, tell WordStar you want to write a memo.	D
15	WordStar asks: NAME OF FILE TO EDIT? WordStar briefly displays the comment NEW FILE, then transports you to the edit mode.	AD.MMO (Press RETURN.)
16	The first thing you want WordStar to do is read in a copy of your special format file.	^ KR
17	WordStar asks: NAME OF FILE TO READ? All your special memo format commands should have appeared at the top of your document.	MEMO.FMT (Press RETURN.)

HOW TO CREATE AND USE A SPECIAL DOCUMENT FORMAT

You Enter . . .	*WordStar Comments and Important Notes*	
(Use cursor-movement commands as necessary.)	Position the cursor on any one of the dashes that makes up your special ruler line.	**18**
^OF	Tell WordStar you want to reset your margins and tabs to match that ruler line. WordStar should have modified the screen ruler line to match the special ruler line you created. If so, you are now ready to type your memo.	**19**
^I (Enter date. Press RETURN as necessary.)	First, tab over and type today's date. Then move the cursor down to begin typing your note.	**20**
(Enter memo.)	Now type the memo you see below.	**21**

```
                              (Date)

Dear Bob:

Sorry,  that  Super  Bowl ad has to go.  Who knows  who
Knute Rockne is anymore?  Remember who our market is- -
find  someone who played in the Super Bowl in the  last
10 years, please!

                              Tom
```

HOW TO CREATE AND USE A SPECIAL DOCUMENT FORMAT

WordStar Comments and Important Notes	*You Enter . . .*
22 Proofread and correct any errors. Then save this memo, exiting WordStar to clear the memo format. If you are going to continue with the exercises, return to WordStar with A:WS.	^ KX

WHAT YOU JUST DID

You have spent a little time now creating a special document format file that will save you a lot of time in the future! From now on, instead of having to modify WordStar's standard format every time you type a memo, you can simply read in a copy of your memo format file.

When you want to create another special document format, follow these steps:

1. Determine the outside dimensions of the paper you plan to use and what the text margins and tabs should be. Then translate these calculations into units of measure that WordStar can understand: lines per vertical inch and columns per horizontal inch.
2. Create a special format file that contains only the appropriate format commands and special ruler line. Save this file.
3. Open a new file and read your special format file into it, using WordStar's command ^ KR.
4. Position the cursor somewhere on the special ruler line and enter the command ^ OF to match the screen ruler line to the one in the format file.
5. Type your document, using the special format.

You can create special format files to print envelopes, adjusting the page length, page offset, and page numbering. You can also create special table formats if you frequently use the same format for columns of figures. Just follow the steps outlined above to determine what format commands you need to use. Sometimes it will take a few tries to get the format just right, but once you succeed you will never have to create that format again.

R
D F G H
X V B N M

PART THREE

MailMerge Applications

#
3
%
^
6
&
7
*
8
E
Y
S
D
F
H
J
C
V
B
N

sixteen

Introduction

MailMerge is a program that works in cooperation with WordStar to cut your typing time by automatically merging information stored in two different files. In this section, we will explain some important MailMerge commands, and describe how to insert them in WordStar files. Then we will walk you through several basic MailMerge applications, so that you can see how easy it is to improve your productivity by using MailMerge shortcuts to produce documents.

WHAT IS MAILMERGE?

Despite what you might think from its name, MailMerge is not a mailing list program. You cannot use MailMerge to create a list of names and addresses or boilerplate paragraphs. Use WordStar or another data-entry program to create these files.

MailMerge provides a set of commands that can be imbedded in WordStar files to tell WordStar where to find the information you want, what that information looks like, and where it should be inserted in your document. When you create a WordStar file to take advantage of MailMerge capabilities, you include the form document (the text that does not change whenever you print it) and imbedded MailMerge commands that define the variable information and point out where the variable information should be inserted.

WHEN TO USE MAILMERGE

You have seen how quickly you can produce standard letters and documents using WordStar. However, if you need to produce many similar letters or documents, the applications we have described still require quite a lot of your time. Using MailMerge makes these applications even quicker and simpler.

You can use MailMerge commands to tell WordStar to insert information provided by an operator before printing, to insert selected information from a master file, or to insert a whole file. For example, you can use MailMerge commands to print many customized versions of a letter, each with a different inside address and salutation. You can also use MailMerge commands to create a document that includes boilerplate paragraphs without reading in copies of the paragraphs, thereby avoiding waste of storage space. When it comes time to print, MailMerge will tell WordStar which paragraphs to include in the document.

HOW MAILMERGE WORKS

Getting Started

MailMerge only functions in cooperation with WordStar. When you purchase the MailMerge program, use your disk operating system's file-copy command to copy the MAILMRGE.OVR file onto your WordStar disk. MAILMRGE.OVR explains MailMerge imbedded commands to WordStar, so that it knows what to do with them.

Having copied the program, you can access MailMerge by selecting the M command found in WordStar's no-file menu.

Using MailMerge Commands

You have already learned how to enter imbedded dot commands in a file in the WordStar applications you have practiced. The MailMerge command format follows the same rules:

1. All MailMerge commands begin with a period.
2. The period must appear in column 1, regardless of the left margin you have set for your text.
3. The period is followed immediately by the appropriate MailMerge command, with no space between the period and the command, or within the command itself.
4. Each command is followed by a space, then additional information that defines the parameters of the command (for example, the name of the file to be merged).

5. Each command must appear on a line by itself. You indicate the end of the command by pressing RETURN after typing the last character in the command.

Normally, these commands are entered at the beginning of the form document so that WordStar can read all the commands before it begins printing. You may enter other WordStar imbedded commands before or after your set of MailMerge commands. For example, you might include the command .OP to omit page numbering on one-page letters.

Assigning Titles and Values to Variables

Each piece of information you want to insert in a form document is called a variable because it changes each time you print the document. When you use MailMerge, you must assign a generic title to each variable. For example, you might use the title SPOUSE to indicate where WordStar should insert the name of the addressee's spouse.

There are rules that limit the types of titles you may use:

1. Each title within the same file must be unique.
2. Each title may be from 1 to 40 characters long. To eliminate a lot of unnecessary typing, keep the titles as short as possible.
3. Each title must begin with a letter. MailMerge does not care if the letter is typed in upper- or lowercase.
4. Within the title, you may include letters, numbers, or hyphens. You may not include any other punctuation marks.
5. Do not include spaces within the title.

In general, choose short titles that will make sense to you later. WordStar does not know or care what the titles mean—it just recognizes each string of characters as a unique symbol specifying a certain type of information. However, you will care if you cannot figure out later on what piece of information you originally thought you wanted to appear.

Although each variable title must be unique so that WordStar knows what information to look for, the value for that title will change every time you print the document. A variable value is the actual text that will be printed in the places you indicate. The title SPOUSE may be replaced by the value Mary, or Tom, or Bob, depending on whose letter is being printed.

The format for variable values is not as limited as the format for titles. A variable value can be from 1 to 200 characters in length. It can begin with and include any letters, numbers, punctuations marks, or symbols.

Inserting Operator-Supplied Information

The first MailMerge command you enter in a file should tell WordStar where to find the information you want to insert. If you want to type in the variable values just before WordStar prints your document, you begin the document by entering the MailMerge command .AV followed by a variable title. This command defines the variable title and indicates that WordStar should ask you for the variable value (AV stands for *ask for value*).

For example, to define the variable SPOUSE, the appropriate MailMerge command would be .AV SPOUSE. Once you have defined the variable title, you enter the word SPOUSE within the document wherever you want WordStar to insert the spouse's name.

How does WordStar know the word SPOUSE should be replaced with a value, and not typed as it appears in the document? Within a document, you flag the title by typing the ampersand, &, before and after the word itself. So the word SPOUSE would be typed &SPOUSE& when entered in a document.

When you implement MailMerge by selecting M from WordStar's no-file menu, WordStar recognizes that every word bracketed by ampersands is a variable title that should be replaced with a value. So when it reads the command .AV SPOUSE, WordStar asks: *SPOUSE?* and expects you to type in the appropriate spouse's name. While printing the document, WordStar would insert the name you typed wherever the word &SPOUSE& appeared in the document.

If you need to supply several variables, just enter a separate .AV command for each title. Remember, each MailMerge command must appear on a line by itself. At print time, WordStar will ask you to provide all the variable values before it begins printing.

Inserting Information from a Data File

If you want to use selected information from a list stored in a separate data file, your first MailMerge command must include the name of that file. Use the command .DF (for *data file*) followed by the file name. For example, the command .DF MAIL.LST indicates that you want to use a data file called MAIL.LST.

If the data file is not stored on the disk in the logged disk drive (which holds your WordStar disk), you must enter the appropriate drive letter or number followed by a colon before the file name. For example, the command .DF B:MAIL.LST tells WordStar that you want to use the data file named MAIL.LST, which is stored on the disk inserted in drive B.

Once you have named your data file, you enter a command or commands to tell WordStar the sequence and titles of the variable values it will find in the data file. Use the command .RV (for *read the following values*) followed by the variable titles in the order in which their values appear in the file. Separate the variable titles with commas, but do not leave spaces between them.

For example, the command .RV NAME,ADDRESS,CITY,STATE,ZIP, PHONE tells WordStar to read the values for the titles NAME, ADDRESS, CITY, STATE, ZIP, and PHONE, which it will find in that order in the data file named in the preceeding .DF command. WordStar will print an individual document for each set of these titles that it finds in the data file. As we mentioned before, the titles must be bracketed by &s within the body of the the form document, so that WordStar knows where to print the values.

When using the .RV command, you must list the titles of the whole set of values stored in a data file, even if you do not intend to use the whole set. WordStar recognizes a value by its position in the file, not by its content. For example, suppose COMPANY NAME is stored between NAME and ADDRESS in the data file. If you entered the command used above, WordStar assumes that the value it finds in the first position is NAME and inserts it wherever the code &NAME& appears in a document. So far so good. However, WordStar then assumes that the value it finds in the second position is ADDRESS, because that is what you told it. Although you know that the value in the second position is really COMPANY NAME, WordStar is not smart enough to figure that out. Wherever it finds the title &ADDRESS&, it will print the second-position value, which is actually COMPANY NAME.

Be sure to name all values in a data file, even if you do not intend to use them. If the set of values in your data file has a long string of variable titles, you may use more than one .RV command to list them all. Just be sure you type all the titles in their correct order. The two commands .RV NAME,ADDRESS,CITY, and .RV STATE,ZIP,PHONE mean the same to WordStar as the one-line command we used above. However, make sure that you follow the last title in the first command with a comma, so that WordStar knows there are more titles to come.

Creating MailMerge Data Files

A MailMerge data file is a list of many different sets of variable values, all entered in the same order. For example, a list of ten names and addresses may be a data file. Each individual's name and address, or set of variable names is called a record.

In order for MailMerge to use a data file, the records must be in a certain format. Some data-entry programs, such as MicroPro's DataStar, automatically create the appropriate format as you enter each record. You can also use WordStar to create a MailMerge data file by opening a file, typing the records in the appropriate format, then saving the file on disk. However, WordStar does not create the format for you, so you have to follow these rules:

1. Each record must appear on a line by itself. After typing the last value in each record, press RETURN to tell WordStar you have completed the record.

2. There may be no carriage returns within the record. It is also a good idea to set very wide margins when typing a MailMerge data file, so that records do not wrap around to a second line.

3. Each value must be separated from the value that follows it by a comma. These commas let WordStar know where one value ends and another begins.

4. If you must use commas within a value (for example, Escape, Inc. as the value COMPANY NAME), put quotation marks on either side of the value text so that WordStar knows that the internal comma does not mark the end of one value and the beginning of another (for example, "Escape, Inc."). The quotation marks will not be printed in the form document.

5. If a particular record does not include all the variables listed in the .RV command, tell WordStar which one is missing by including an extra comma in the appropriate position. For example, if one addressee has no company name in the second position, you enter NAME,,ADDRESS,CITY,STATE,ZIP, PHONE. WordStar will count the commas to locate the next value.

Another reminder, when entering the .RV command that lists the variable titles of the values in a data file, be sure to list the whole set of titles, even if you do not intend to use them all in your document.

Inserting Boilerplate Paragraphs

If you want to insert a whole boilerplate paragraph that is stored in its own file into your document, your first MailMerge command will include the name of that file. Use the command .FI (for *file insert*) followed by the file name. For example, to insert boilerplate paragraph 2, which you created in section *Eight,* use the command .FI 2.

If the file is not stored on the disk inserted in the logged disk drive (the disk that holds WordStar), you must enter the appropriate drive letter followed by a colon before the file name (for example, .FI B:2).

WHAT EQUIPMENT AND SKILLS DO YOU NEED?

In order to try these exercises, you must have an operational computer system, including a printer. You must have a version of WordStar that will work on that system, and your WordStar disk must contain the MailMerge program file called MAILMRGE.OVR.

If you skipped any of the WordStar exercises, you may have to do a little extra typing before you can try out the MailMerge applications. Specifically, you will need:

1. A copy of the file called CONTRACT.AIR, used in section *Six;*
2. A copy of the file called INQUIRY.LTR, used in section *Seven;* and
3. Copies of boilerplate-paragraph files 1 through 8, used in section *Eight.*

We chose to reuse these files to cut your typing time, and also to show you how much time you can save performing the same operations with MailMerge.

By now, you should also be able to boot the system and move from DOS to WordStar's no-file menu, and be comfortable entering and editing text so that you can correct any typographical errors you may make. You should also have read and understood the MailMerge concepts and rules explained in this introduction. We will tell you anything else you need to know as we go along.

3
%
^ 6
& 7
* 8
E
Y
S
D
F
H
J
C
V
B
N

seventeen

Form Documents Using Operator-supplied Values

WHEN TO USE MAILMERGE FOR FORM DOCUMENTS

In section *Six,* you learned how to create a standard contract called CONTRACT.AIR that could be customized for different charterers and air carriers. Within the document, you typed in a unique symbol wherever you wanted the name of either party to appear.

When you were ready to customize the document, you used WordStar's search and replace capability to find each symbol and replace it with the appropriate company name. The special symbols were thus the equivalent of MailMerge's variable titles, while the names ESCAPE and SPACE-WARP were the equivalent of variable values. Once the names were inserted, you had to move through the document to reformat the text within the margins, because the variable values were much longer than the variable titles.

Using MailMerge instead of WordStar, you can eliminate that final reformatting step. When MailMerge inserts the names, it also reformats the paragraphs to fit your margin settings.

WHAT YOU WILL DO

First you will read in a copy of CONTRACT.AIR, the file you created in section *Six*. Then you will enter the appropriate .AV commands so that WordStar will ask you to supply the names of the charterer and air carrier before it prints your document. Next you will replace the original * and # you used within the document as search and replace symbols with the appropriate MailMerge variable titles. Finally, you will save the form document, select M from WordStar's no-file menu, and print a customized version by typing the specific variable values when WordStar asks you for them.

HOW TO CREATE A MAILMERGE FORM DOCUMENT

	WordStar Comments and Important Notes	***You Enter . . .***
1	When the no-file menu appears on the screen, tell WordStar you want to create a new file.	D
2	WordStar asks: NAME OF FILE TO EDIT? WordStar flashes the message NEW FILE, then transports you to the edit mode.	AVCNTRCT.AIR (Press RETURN.)
3	When the edit-mode main menu appears on the screen, tell WordStar you want to read in a copy of a file.	^ KR
4	WordStar asks: NAME OF FILE TO READ?	CONTRACT.AIR (Press RETURN.)

HOW TO CREATE A MAILMERGE FORM DOCUMENT

You Enter . . .	*WordStar Comments and Important Notes*
	If nothing appears and WordStar advises: FILE A:CONTRACT.AIR NOT FOUND, perhaps you are logged on to drive A and the file is stored on the disk in drive B. If so, either enter B:CONTRACT.AIR to tell WordStar to look for the file in drive B, or log on to drive B and give the same command again. The following file should appear on your screen.

```
THIS  AGREEMENT IS ENTERED INTO by the carrier,  herein described
as * and the chartering organization, herein described as #.

The  carrier, *,   agrees to abide by the applicable  rules  and
regulations established by the International Aerospace Consortium
of 1983 in the operation of the described flight.

*  further  agrees to reserve 15 passenger seats for the  express
use of passengers approved and contracted by #. * guarantees that
these seats include life-support equipment capable of  sustaining
passenger viability for a minimum of 6 months at sublight speeds.

When   assigning  these  seats,   #  ensures  that  all  ticketed
passengers have met or exceeded the Minimum Physical Requirements
for Passengers Attempting Extended Space Travel,  as outlined  in
IAC regulation 14.2.1a.

*  undertakes  to use its best efforts to carry # passengers  and
baggage  with reasonable dispatch.  Times shown in timetables  or
elsewhere are not guaranteed,  and form no part of this contract.
Return passage is not guaranteed.  By accepting this Agreement, #
confirms   that  it  will  present  approved  waivers  from   all
passengers  indicating  their understanding of  these  terms  and
resigning  all rights to litigation by themselves and their heirs
in  the  event  that  * is unable to complete  the  flight  in  a
satisfactory manner.
.OP
```

HOW TO CREATE A MAILMERGE FORM DOCUMENT

	WordStar Comments and Important Notes	*You Enter . . .*
5	Begin by positioning the cursor in column 1 of line 1, and adding a couple of blank lines to the top of the document.	(Use cursor-movement commands as necessary.) ^N^N
6	With the cursor positioned in column 1 of line 1, tell WordStar the titles of the variables you are going to use. Enter the first variable title command, remembering that the period must appear in column 1.	.AV CARRIER (Press RETURN.)
7	With the cursor positioned in column 1 of line 2, enter the next variable title command. So far, you have told WordStar to ask you or another operator to supply the values for the variables entitled CARRIER and CHARTERER. Now you need to replace the carrier symbol * that you used before with the appropriate MailMerge title.	.AV CHARTERER (Press RETURN.)
8	Tell WordStar you want to search and replace quickly.	^ QA

HOW TO CREATE A MAILMERGE FORM DOCUMENT

You Enter . . .	*WordStar Comments and Important Notes*	
* (Press RETURN.)	WordStar asks: FIND?	**9**
&CARRIER& (Press RETURN.)	WordStar asks: REPLACE WITH?	**10**
GN (Press RETURN.)	WordStar asks: OPTIONS? (? FOR INFO) Tell WordStar to replace globally, without asking for your approval. WordStar should move through your entire file, replacing every * with the MailMerge code &CARRIER&.	**11**
^ QA	With the cursor still positioned at the bottom of your document, tell Word-Star you want to find and replace another symbol.	**12**
# (Press RETURN.)	WordStar asks: FIND?	**13**
&CHARTERER& (Press RETURN.)	WordStar asks: REPLACE WITH?	**14**

HOW TO CREATE A MAILMERGE FORM DOCUMENT

	WordStar Comments and Important Notes	*You Enter . . .*
15	WordStar asks: OPTIONS? (? FOR INFO) Tell WordStar to search backwards and replace globally, without asking for your approval. WordStar should have moved back to the beginning of the document, replacing every # it found along the way.	BGN (Press RETURN.)
16	Now you have to reformat the document, so that WordStar knows how you want the finished document to look.	^ QQ ^ B
17	Once the cursor reaches the bottom of the document, add the page-break command. (The omit-page-number command, .OP, should already be there. If it is not, add that, too.)	.PA (Press RETURN.)
18	Your finished form document should look like the one on the next page.	(Compare texts.)
19	If everything looks correct, save this file.	^ KD

```
.AV CARRIER
.AV CHARTERER

THIS AGREEMENT IS ENTERED INTO by the carrier, herein described
as &CARRIER&, and the chartering organization, herein described
as &CHARTERER&.

The carrier, &CARRIER&, agrees to abide by the applicable rules
and regulations established by the International Aerospace
Consortium of 1983 in the operation of the described flight.

&CARRIER& further agrees to reserve 15 passenger seats for the
express use of passengers approved and contracted by &CHARTERER&.
&CARRIER& guarantees that these seats include life-support
equipment capable of sustaining passenger viability for a minimum
of 6 months at sublight speeds.

When assigning these seats, &CHARTERER& ensures that all ticketed
passengers have met or exceeded the Minimum Physical Requirements
for Passengers Attempting Extended Space Travel, as outlined in
IAC regulation 14.2.1a.

&CARRIER& undertakes to use its best efforts to carry &CHARTERER&
passengers and baggage with reasonable dispatch. Times shown in
timetables or elsewhere are not guaranteed, and form no part of
this contract. Return passage is not guaranteed. By accepting
this Agreement, &CHARTERER& confirms that it will present
approved waivers from all passengers indicating their
understanding of these terms and resigning all rights to
litigation by themselves and their heirs in the event that
&CARRIER& is unable to complete the flight in a satisfactory
manner.

.OP
.PA
```

HOW TO CREATE A MAILMERGE FORM DOCUMENT

	WordStar Comments and Important Notes	*You Enter . . .*
1	When the no-file menu appears on the screen, prepare your printer.	(Turn on printer. Insert paper.)
2	Tell WordStar you are ready to merge-print a file.	M
3	WordStar asks: NAME OF FILE TO MERGE-PRINT?	AVCNTRCT.AIR (Press ESC.)
4	WordStar flashes P = STOP PRINT, then asks: CARRIER?	SPACE-WARP (Press RETURN.)
5	WordStar asks: CHARTERER?	ESCAPE (Press RETURN.)
6	WordStar prints your contract, filling in the appropriate names where indicated in the file. Your contract should look like the one on the facing page.	(Compare contracts.)

THIS AGREEMENT IS ENTERED INTO by the carrier, herein described as SPACE-WARP, and the chartering organization, herein described as ESCAPE.

The carrier, SPACE-WARP, agrees to abide by the applicable rules and regulations established by the International Aerospace Consortium of 1983 in the operation of the described flight.

SPACE-WARP further agrees to reserve 15 passenger seats for the express use of passengers approved and contracted by ESCAPE. SPACE-WARP guarantees that these seats include life-support equipment capable of sustaining passenger viability for a minimum of 6 months at sublight speeds.

When assigning these seats, ESCAPE ensures that all ticketed passengers have met or exceeded the Minimum Physical Requirements for Passengers Attempting Extended Space Travel, as outlined in IAC regulation 14.2.1a.

SPACE-WARP undertakes to use its best efforts to carry ESCAPE passengers and baggage with reasonable dispatch. Times shown in timetables or elsewhere are not guaranteed, and form no part of this contract. Return passage is not guaranteed. By accepting this Agreement, ESCAPE confirms that it will present approved waivers from all passengers indicating their understanding of these terms and resigning all rights to litigation by themselves or their heirs in the event that SPACE-WARP is unable to complete the flight in a satisfactory manner.

WHAT YOU JUST DID

You have just created a form document that you can use over and over again, just by supplying the appropriate variable values when asked. Unlike the method described in section *Six*, you do not have to store individually customized copies of the form document on a disk, wasting important space. WordStar, with the help of MailMerge, inserts the unique values at print time.

These are the steps you should take to prepare a MailMerge form document:

1. Begin the form document by defining the variable titles of the values WordStar should ask for at print time, using the MailMerge command .AV followed by the title. List each variable in a separate .AV command.

2. Type the body of the document, entering the MailMerge code &TITLE& wherever you want a defined value to appear.

3. Save the form document file, then customize it by selecting M from WordStar's no-file menu when you want to print a customized version.

4. Enter the values for the variable titles as WordStar asks you for them.

3
%
^ 6
& 7
* 8
E
Y
S
D
F
H
J
C
V
B
N

eighteen
Form Letters Using Operator-supplied Values

WHEN TO USE MAILMERGE FOR FORM LETTERS

As noted in section *Seven,* it is much easier to use MailMerge to generate form letters than it is to use WordStar, which involves cutting and pasting to reproduce the inside address on the envelope. Although having WordStar ask you for the information is only one step better than copying address blocks from place to place, it is a significant step better. In section *Twenty,* we will show you how to print lots of form letters even more easily.

WHAT YOU WILL DO

First, you will open a new file and read in a copy of the form letter called INQUIRY.LTR that you created in section *Seven.* You will modify this letter by adding MailMerge .AV commands to tell WordStar to ask you or another operator for the variable values at print time. Then you will add the MailMerge &TITLE& codes within the letter and envelope format, so that WordStar knows where to insert the values. Finally, you will save the letter, then print a customized copy using the merge-print command M.

HOW TO CREATE A MAILMERGE FORM LETTER

	WordStar Comments and Important Notes	***You Enter . . .***
1	When the no-file menu appears on the screen, tell WordStar you want to create a new file.	D
2	WordStar asks: NAME OF FILE TO EDIT? WordStar flashes the message NEW FILE, then transports you to the edit mode.	AVINQRY.LTR (Press RETURN.)
3	When the edit-mode main menu appears on the screen, tell WordStar you want to read in a copy of a file.	^ KR
4	WordStar asks: NAME OF FILE TO READ? If nothing appears, and WordStar advises: FILE A:INQUIRY.LTR NOT FOUND, perhaps you are logged on to drive A and the file is stored on the disk in drive B. If so, either enter B:INQUIRY.LTR to tell WordStar to look for the file in drive B, or log on to drive B and give the same command again. The file opposite should appear on your screen.	INQUIRY.LTR (Press RETURN.)
5	Begin by positioning the cursor in column 1 of line 1, and adding a few blank lines to the top of the document.	(Use cursor-movement commands as necessary.) ^ N ^ N ^ N ^ N ^ N

```
.OP
                                   *


*

Dear *:

Thank you for applying for a seat on ESCAPE's first space flight.

Enclosed  you  will find all the necessary documents required  by
Space-Warp  Airways  and the International Aerospace  Consortium.
These forms must be completed and returned by January 1, 1984, in
order for you to be eligible for consideration. Be sure to follow
the instructions outlined in the attached 350-page guide.

In  particular,  please be sure your personal therapist completes
the  orange  psychological-profile form,  listing all  known  and
suspected neuroses, psychoses, and possible paranoid fantasies.

Also be sure that all your former employers,  family members, and
friends  complete  the attached compatibility  questionnaires  to
ensure that all 15 of our passengers are capable of creating  and
sustaining  a  pleasant  and productive  environment  during  our
travel through time and space.

ESCAPE  looks forward to welcoming you aboard our first flight to
the stars.

                       Sincerely,


                       Spock Rogers
                       Quality Control Specialist


Enclosure
.PA
```

HOW TO CREATE A MAILMERGE FORM LETTER

WordStar Comments and Important Notes	*You Enter . . .*
6 With the cursor still positioned in column 1 of line 1, tell WordStar the titles of the variables you are going to use. Enter the first variable title command, remembering that the period must appear in column 1.	.AV DATE (Press RETURN.)
7 With the cursor positioned in column 1 of line 2, enter a variable title command for the addressee's first name.	.AV FNAME (Press RETURN.)
8 With the cursor positioned in column 1 of each succeeding line, enter the rest of the variable title commands listed. Be sure that each command appears on a line by itself, with the command period appearing in column 1. You have now told WordStar to ask you to supply the values for seven different variables. Now you need to use the special symbol * to find the right spot to enter the variable titles into the document.	.AV LNAME (Press RETURN.) .AV STREET (Press RETURN.) .AV CITY (Press RETURN.) .AV STATE (Press RETURN.) .AV ZIP (Press RETURN.)
9 Use WordStar's search and replace command to find the *s so that you can replace them with blanks and enter the variable titles.	^QA

HOW TO CREATE A MAILMERGE FORM LETTER

You Enter . . .	*WordStar Comments and Important Notes*	
* (Press RETURN.)	WordStar asks: FIND?	10
(Press RETURN.)	WordStar asks: REPLACE WITH?	11
N (Press RETURN.)	WordStar asks: OPTIONS? (? FOR INFO) WordStar moves to the first *, deletes it, then waits for new instructions.	12
^ V (If necessary.)	First make sure that INSERT is ON.	13
&DATE& ^ L	This is where you want the date to appear, so enter the appropriate MailMerge title code, then tell WordStar to find the next *, using ^ L. WordStar skips to the * that marks the beginning of the inside address, deletes it, then waits for new instructions.	14
&FNAME& &LNAME& (Press RETURN.)	Enter the first and last name codes. Be sure to leave a space between them, so a space is printed between first and last names.	15

HOW TO CREATE A MAILMERGE FORM LETTER

	WordStar Comments and Important Notes	***You Enter . . .***
16	Now enter the appropriate MailMerge codes for the rest of the inside address. Be sure to type them exactly as shown, including the spaces and commas indicated. End the entry by telling WordStar to look for the next *. WordStar moves to, and deletes, the * marking the salutation.	&STREET& (Press RETURN.) &CITY&, &STATE& &ZIP& ^ L
17	Type in the appropriate MailMerge code, then tell WordStar to skip to the next *, which marks the envelope address.	&FNAME& ^ L
18	Now duplicate the envelope address format, using MailMerge titles in place of actual variables values.	&FNAME& &LNAME& (Press RETURN.) &STREET& (Press RETURN.) &CITY&, &STATE& &ZIP& (Press RETURN.)
19	Your letter should look like the one on the next page.	(Compare letters.)
20	If everything looks correct, save this file.	^ KD

```
.OP
.AV DATE
.AV FNAME
.AV LNAME
.AV STREET
.AV CITY
.AV STATE
.AV ZIP
                              &DATE&


&FNAME& &LNAME&
&STREET&
&CITY&, &STATE& &ZIP&

Dear &FNAME&:

Thank you for applying for a seat on ESCAPE's first space flight.

Enclosed  you will find all the necessary documents  required  by
Space-Warp  Airways  and the International Aerospace  Consortium.
These forms must be completed and returned by January 1, 1984, in
order for you to be eligible for consideration. Be sure to follow
the instructions outlined in the attached 350-page guide.

In particular,  please be sure your personal therapist  completes
the  orange  psychological-profile form,  listing all  known  and
suspected neuroses, psychoses, and possible paranoid fantasies.

Also be sure that all your former employers,  family members, and
friends  complete  the attached compatibility  questionnaires  to
ensure  that all 15 of our passengers are capable of creating and
sustaining  a  pleasant  and productive  environment  during  our
travel through time and space.

ESCAPE looks forward to welcoming you aboard our first flight  to
the stars.

                              Sincerely,


                              Spock Rogers
                              Quality Control Specialist

Enclosure

.PA

                             &FNAME& &LNAME&
                             &STREET&
                             &CITY&, &STATE& &ZIP&
```

HOW TO CUSTOMIZE A MAILMERGE FORM LETTER

	WordStar Comments and Important Notes	*You Enter . . .*
1	When the no-file menu appears on the screen, prepare your printer.	(Turn on printer. Insert paper.)
2	Tell WordStar you are ready to merge-print a file.	M
3	WordStar asks: NAME OF FILE TO MERGE-PRINT? Press RETURN instead of ESCAPE because you want to give WordStar another instruction.	AVINQRY.LTR (Press RETURN.)
4	WordStar asks: DISK FILE OUTPUT	(Press RETURN.)
5	WordStar asks: START AT PAGE NUMBER	(Press RETURN.)
6	WordStar asks: STOP AFTER PAGE NUMBER	(Press RETURN.)
7	WordStar asks: NUMBER OF COPIES	(Press RETURN.)

HOW TO CUSTOMIZE A MAILMERGE FORM LETTER

You Enter . . .	WordStar Comments and Important Notes	
(Press RETURN.)	WordStar asks: USE FORM FEEDS	8
(Press RETURN.)	WordStar asks: SUPPRESS PAGE FORMATTING	9
Y (Press RETURN.)	WordStar asks: PAUSE FOR PAPER CHANGE BETWEEN PAGES	10
(Press RETURN.)	WordStar advises: Ready printer, press RETURN.	11
October 14, 1983 (Press RETURN.)	WordStar flashes P= STOP PRINT, then asks: DATE?	12
Ricky (Press RETURN.)	WordStar asks: FNAME?	13
Lindstrom (Press RETURN.)	WordStar asks: LNAME?	14
1234 Analog Way (Press RETURN.)	WordStar asks: STREET?	15

HOW TO CUSTOMIZE A MAILMERGE FORM LETTER

WordStar Comments and Important Notes	*You Enter . . .*
16 WordStar asks: CITY?	Stereo City (Press RETURN.)
17 WordStar asks: STATE?	CA (Press RETURN.)
18 WordStar asks: ZIP? WordStar prints your letter, filling in the appropriate information where indicated in the file.	94578 (Press RETURN.)
19 Having printed the letter, WordStar pauses for you to remove the paper and insert an envelope. Then tell WordStar to continue printing.	(Remove letter. Insert and align envelope.) P
20 Your letter and envelope should look like those opposite.	(Compare letter and envelope.)

October 14, 1983

Ricky Lindstrom
1234 Analog Way
Stereo City, CA 94578

Dear Ricky:

Thank you for applying for a seat on ESCAPE's first space flight.

Enclosed you will find all the necessary documents required by Space-Warp Airways and the International Aerospace Consortium. These forms must be completed and returned by January 1, 1984, in order for you to be eligible for consideration. Be sure to follow the instructions outlined in the attached 350-page guide.

In particular, please be sure your personal therapist completes the orange psychological-profile form, listing all known and suspected neuroses, psychoses, and possible paranoid fantasies.

Also be sure that all your former employers, family members, and friends complete the attached compatibility questionnaires to ensure that all 15 of our passengers are capable of creating and sustaining a pleasant and productive environment during our travel through time and space.

ESCAPE looks forward to welcoming you aboard our first flight to the stars.

Sincerely,

Spock Rogers
Quality Control Specialist

Enclosure

Ricky Lindstrom
1234 Analog Way
Stereo City, CA 94578

WHAT YOU JUST DID

You have just created a form letter format into which different names and addresses can be inserted at the operator's whim. Notice that you have not wasted disk space by storing multiple customized copies of the letter. Whenever you need to send this letter to a new customer, follow these steps:

1. Select M from WordStar's no-file menu.
2. Enter the form-letter file name.
3. Fill in the appropriate values when asked for them. WordStar and MailMerge will take care of the rest!

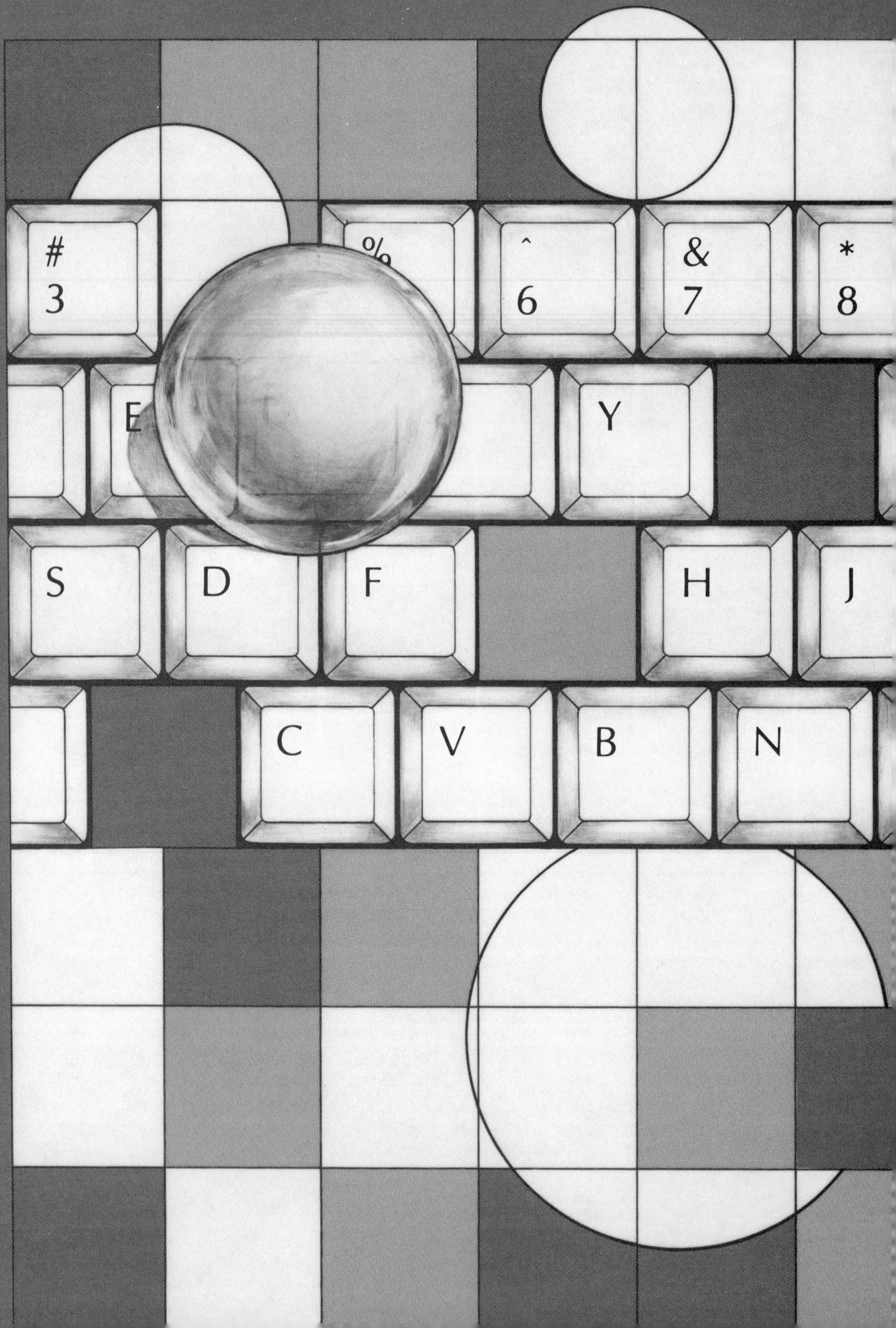

#
3
6
&
7
*
8
E
Y
S
D
F
H
J
C
V
B
N

nineteen
Form Documents Using a Data File

WHEN TO USE DATA FILES WITH FORM DOCUMENTS

In section *Seventeen,* you learned how much easier it is to use MailMerge to customize a form document than to search and replace with WordStar commands. However, though it is no problem to type in two variable values when asked for them, how boring and time consuming this would be if you needed to type five or ten contracts one right after the other!

When you need to customize more than one letter, it is best to create a data file that holds all the variable values. If you insert the correct commands at the beginning of the document, WordStar will be able to pick out the right names to plug into each contract. If your printer uses continuous form paper, you will not even have to stand around and wait for the contracts to print. Go to lunch—and when you come back, they will all be perfectly printed!

WHAT YOU WILL DO

First, you will create a data file that holds the set of variable values you want to include in the contract. You will save this file.

Next, you will open a new file and read in a copy of the document you created in section *Seventeen,* called AVCNTRCT.AIR. Then you will delete the .AV commands that you used to tell WordStar to ask the operator for the variable values, and will replace them with the appropriate data file commands. You will save this file.

Finally, you will put both files together, using WordStar's M command. You will produce two different contracts for two sets of customers, both perfectly printed.

HOW TO CREATE A MAILMERGE DATA FILE

WordStar Comments and Important Notes	*You Enter . . .*
1 When the no-file menu is displayed on the screen, tell WordStar you want to create a new document.	D
2 WordStar asks: NAME OF FILE TO EDIT? WordStar flashes the comment NEW FILE, then transports you to the edit mode.	PARTIES.CNT (Press RETURN.)
3 Enter the list you see below. These individual records list the names of the parties that will be inserted into a form contract. Enter them one per line, exactly as you see them. Type a comma between each value, and end each record by pressing RETURN. If a comma appears within the body of a value, enclose the value in quotation marks.	(Enter text.)
4 All done? That wasn't too difficult, was it? Save this file.	^ KD

```
SPACE-WARP,ESCAPE,"JULY 4, 1984" (Press RETURN.)
GLOBAL,ESCAPE,"JULY 4, 1985" (Press RETURN.)
```

HOW TO USE A DATA FILE TO CUSTOMIZE A FORM DOCUMENT

You Enter . . .	*WordStar Comments and Important Notes*	
D	When the no-file menu is displayed on the screen, tell WordStar you want to create or edit a document.	**1**
DFCNTRCT.AIR (Press RETURN.)	WordStar asks: NAME OF FILE TO EDIT? WordStar flashes NEW FILE, then transports you to the edit mode.	**2**
^ KR	When the edit-mode main menu appears on the screen, tell WordStar you want to read in a copy of a file.	**3**
AVCNTRCT.AIR (Press RETURN.)	WordStar asks: NAME OF FILE TO READ?	**4**

HOW TO USE A DATA FILE TO CUSTOMIZE A FORM DOCUMENT

WordStar Comments and Important Notes	*You Enter . . .*
5 The file that appears on your screen is the one you created in section *Seventeen.* It should look like this:	(Compare contracts.)

```
.AV CARRIER
.AV CHARTERER

THIS  AGREEMENT IS ENTERED INTO by the carrier,  herein described
as &CARRIER&,  and the chartering organization,  herein described
as &CHARTERER&.

The carrier,  &CARRIER&,  agrees to abide by the applicable rules
and  regulations  established  by  the  International  Aerospace
Consortium of 1983 in the operation of the described flight.

&CARRIER&  further  agrees to reserve 15 passenger seats for  the
express use of passengers approved and contracted by &CHARTERER&.
&CARRIER&  guarantees  that  these  seats  include  life-support
equipment capable of sustaining passenger viability for a minimum
of 6 months at sublight speeds.

When assigning these seats, &CHARTERER& ensures that all ticketed
passengers have met or exceeded the Minimum Physical Requirements
for  Passengers Attempting Extended Space Travel,  as outlined in
IAC regulation 14.2.1a.

&CARRIER& undertakes to use its best efforts to carry &CHARTERER&
passengers and baggage with reasonable dispatch.  Times shown  in
timetables  or elsewhere are not guaranteed,  and form no part of
this  contract.  Return passage is not guaranteed.  By  accepting
this  Agreement,  &CHARTERER&  confirms  that  it  will  present
approved  waivers  from  all  passengers  indicating  their
understanding  of  these  terms  and  resigning  all  rights  to
litigation  by  themselves  and  their heirs in  the  event  that
&CARRIER&  is  unable to complete the flight  in  a  satisfactory
manner.

.OP
.PA
```

HOW TO USE A DATA FILE TO CUSTOMIZE A FORM DOCUMENT

You Enter . . .	*WordStar Comments and Important Notes*	
^Y^Y	First you want to delete the .AV commands, so that you can replace them with the appropriate file commands. Position the cursor on the period of the first .AV command. Then delete that line and the one that follows it.	**6**
.DF PARTIES.CNT (Press RETURN.)	With the cursor still positioned in column 1 of line 1, enter the MailMerge command that tells WordStar the name of the data file you want it to use.	**7**
.RV CARRIER (Press RETURN.) .RV CHARTERER (Press RETURN.) .RV FLIGHT (Press RETURN.)	With the cursor now positioned in *column 1* of line 2, enter the MailMerge command that describes the titles and order of the values found in the data file you just named. Notice that you had to list the flight date as one of the .RV commands, even though you will not use FLIGHT in this contract. Remember, you must list every value that appears in a data file, so that WordStar can count correctly to the values you need. Because you are modifying a copy of a contract already prepared for MailMerge, you do not have to enter the &TITLE& codes within the document—they are already there.	**8**

HOW TO USE A DATA FILE TO CUSTOMIZE A FORM DOCUMENT

WordStar Comments and Important Notes	*You Enter . . .*
9 This is what your contract should now look like:	(Compare contracts.)

```
.DF PARTIES.CNT
.RV CARRIER,
.RV CHARTERER,
.RV FLIGHT

THIS  AGREEMENT IS ENTERED INTO by the carrier,  herein described
as &CARRIER&,  and the chartering organization,  herein described
as &CHARTERER&.

The carrier,  &CARRIER&,  agrees to abide by the applicable rules
and  regulations  established  by  the  International   Aerospace
Consortium of 1983 in the operation of the described flight.

&CARRIER&  further  agrees to reserve 15 passenger seats for  the
express use of passengers approved and contracted by &CHARTERER&.
&CARRIER&  guarantees  that  these  seats  include  life-support
equipment capable of sustaining passenger viability for a minimum
of 6 months at sublight speeds.

When assigning these seats, &CHARTERER& ensures that all ticketed
passengers have met or exceeded the Minimum Physical Requirements
for  Passengers Attempting Extended Space Travel,  as outlined in
IAC regulation 14.2.1a.

&CARRIER& undertakes to use its best efforts to carry &CHARTERER&
passengers and baggage with reasonable dispatch.  Times shown  in
timetables  or elsewhere are not guaranteed,  and form no part of
this  contract.  Return passage is not guaranteed.  By  accepting
this  Agreement,   &CHARTERER&  confirms  that  it  will  present
approved   waivers   from   all   passengers   indicating   their
understanding  of  these  terms  and  resigning  all  rights   to
litigation  by  themselves  and  their heirs in  the  event  that
&CARRIER&  is  unable to complete the flight  in  a  satisfactory
manner.

.OP
.PA
```

HOW TO USE A DATA FILE TO CUSTOMIZE A FORM DOCUMENT

You Enter . . .	*WordStar Comments and Important Notes*	
^ KD	Save this new contract.	**10**
(Turn on printer. Insert paper.)	Since you listed two records in your data file, when the no-file menu reappears on the screen, insert continuous-form paper in your printer.	**11**
M	Tell WordStar you want to merge-print a file.	**12**
DFCNTRCT.AIR (Press ESC.)	WordStar asks: NAME OF FILE TO MERGE-PRINT? Your contract includes directions for finding the right data file, so you do not need to give the data file name. WordStar prints your first contract, using the names SPACE-WARP and ESCAPE. The command .PA tells it to move to the next page. Then it prints a second contract, using the names GLOBAL and ESCAPE.	**13**

WHAT YOU JUST DID

You have just created a MailMerge data file and a compatible MailMerge form document and combined (or merged) them to produce customized contracts. By entering all the variable values in the data file and then turning the customizing process over to WordStar, you freed yourself to do other things.

To use this time-saving technique, follow these steps:

1. Create a data file, listing all the records you want to include in the form document and save it.

2. Create a form document. Begin with the command .DF followed by the name of your data file.

3. On the next line, enter the command .RV followed by the titles of all the values that appear in each record of your data file. Include all the variable titles, even though you may not want to use them all in this document.

4. Insert &TITLE& codes within the body of the document wherever you want the corresponding values from your data file to appear.

5. When you are going to print more than one document, be sure to include the page-break command .PA at the end of the form document, so that the second and succeeding copies begin at the top of a page.

6. Always add the command .OP or the command .PN 1 to the bottom of the document. Use .OP to omit page numbers on one-page documents. Use .PN 1 at the bottom of the first page of a multi-page document, so the second and succeeding copies all begin with a page 1.

7. Save the document file.

8. Turn on the printer and insert continuous-form paper.

9. Use the command M to tell WordStar you want to merge-print a file, give the name of your form document file, and press ESCAPE.

10. Now go and do something else while WordStar goes to work!

#
3
^
6
&
7
*
8
Y
S
D
F
H
J
C
V
B
N

twenty

Form Letters Using a Data File

WHEN TO USE DATA FILES WITH FORM LETTERS

In section *Eighteen,* you customized a form letter using operator-supplied variable values. While that method is a real time-saver for one or two letters, it is extremely tedious when you want to print many letters. In this exercise, we show you how to eliminate this tedium by creating a data file from which WordStar can take all the names and addresses it needs.

WHAT YOU WILL DO

First, you will create a data file, listing all the names and addresses you want to insert in your form letter.

Next, you will open another file and read in a copy of the form letter called AVINQRY.LTR that you created in section *Eighteen.* You will delete the .AV commands that told WordStar to ask you for the names and addresses, and will replace them with the appropriate data file commands.

When you have a lot of letters to type, it is easier to print all the letters first, and then print the envelopes. So you will create a third document file that holds only the format for the envelopes.

When you have created all these files, you will use WordStar's M command to print all the letters, then all the matching envelopes.

HOW TO USE A DATA FILE TO CUSTOMIZE FORM LETTERS

	WordStar Comments and Important Notes	You Enter . . .
1	When the no-file menu appears on the screen, tell WordStar you want to create a new file.	D
2	WordStar asks: NAME OF FILE TO EDIT? WordStar flashes the message NEW FILE, then transports you to the edit mode.	NAMES.LST (Press RETURN.)
3	When the edit-mode main menu appears on the screen, enter the records you see below exactly as they appear. Make sure commas are properly placed between each value in a record.	(Enter text.)
4	Save this file.	^ KD

```
Regis,Hastur,653 St. Valentine's Place,Armida,VA,19090
Lew,Alton,14 Plateau,Aldaran,OR,98734
Jeff,Kerwin,78 Alrinn Avenue,Darkover,NM,93820
```

HOW TO USE A DATA FILE TO CUSTOMIZE FORM LETTERS

You Enter . . .	*WordStar Comments and Important Notes*	
D	When the no-file menu reappears on the screen, tell WordStar you want to create another file.	**5**
DFINQRY.LTR (Press RETURN.)	WordStar asks: NAME OF FILE TO EDIT? WordStar will transport you to the edit mode.	**6**
^ KR	Now tell WordStar you want to read in a copy of an existing file.	**7**
AVINQRY.LTR (Press RETURN.)	WordStar asks: NAME OF FILE TO READ?	**8**

HOW TO USE A DATA FILE TO CUSTOMIZE FORM LETTERS

	WordStar Comments and Important Notes	***You Enter . . .***
9	The form letter you created in section *Eighteen* should appear on your screen as you see it opposite.	(Compare letters.)
10	Position the cursor on the first .AV command, which reads .AV DATE. Delete it and the six .AV commands that follow it.	^ Y (Seven times.)
11	With the cursor still positioned in column 1 of line 2, enter the MailMerge command that tells WordStar the name of the data file where it will find the variable values.	.DF NAMES.LST (Press RETURN.)
12	With the cursor positioned in column 1 of line 3, enter the MailMerge command that defines the titles and order of all the values in your data file. If necessary, use two commands. Just be sure to end the last variable in the first command with a comma.	.RV FNAME,LNAME, (Press RETURN.) .RV STREET, (Press RETURN.) .RV CITY,STATE,ZIP (Press RETURN.)
13	Replace the form letter's &DATE& entry with a real date. You will have to remember to change this date every time you use this form letter. Move the cursor to the first character in the variable title &DATE&. Then delete it.	(Use cursor-movement commands as necessary.) ^ T

```
.OP
.AV DATE
.AV FNAME
.AV LNAME
.AV STREET
.AV CITY
.AV STATE
.AV ZIP
                                   &DATE&

&FNAME& &LNAME&
&STREET&
&CITY&, &STATE& &ZIP&

Dear &FNAME&:

Thank you for applying for a seat on ESCAPE's first space flight.

Enclosed  you  will find all the necessary documents required  by
Space-Warp  Airways and the International  Aerospace  Consortium.
These forms must be completed and returned by January 1, 1984, in
order for you to be eligible for consideration. Be sure to follow
the instructions outlined in the attached 350-page guide.

In  particular,  please be sure your personal therapist completes
the  orange  psychological-profile form,  listing all  known  and
suspected neuroses, psychoses, and possible paranoid fantasies.

Also be sure that all your former employers,  family members, and
friends  complete  the attached compatibility  questionnaires  to
ensure that all 15 of our passengers are capable of creating  and
sustaining  a  pleasant  and productive  environment  during  our
travel through time and space.

ESCAPE  looks forward to welcoming you aboard our first flight to
the stars.

                             Sincerely,


                             Spock Rogers
                             Quality Control Specialist

Enclosure

.PA

                            &FNAME& &LNAME&
                            &STREET&
                            &CITY&, &STATE& &ZIP&
```

HOW TO USE A DATA FILE TO CUSTOMIZE FORM LETTERS

	WordStar Comments and Important Notes	*You Enter . . .*
14	With the cursor still at the position where &DATE& used to be, enter a date.	October 14, 1983
15	You do not need to insert &TITLE& codes within the letter—they are already there. However, you do want to eliminate the envelope format at the bottom of the form letter, because you are going to create a separate file to print envelopes. So move the cursor to the line just below the command .PA that completes the letter page.	(Use cursor-movement commands as necessary.)
16	Now delete everything from the cursor position through the end of the file, so that there is nothing left in this file but the form letter.	^ Y (As necessary.)
17	Your letter should now look like the one opposite.	(Compare letters.)
18	Look good? Save this file.	^ KD
19	When the no-file menu reappears on the screen, tell WordStar you want to create another file.	D

```
.OP
.DF NAMES.LST
.RV FNAME,LNAME,
.RV STREET,
.RV CITY,STATE,ZIP

                                   October 14, 1983


&FNAME& &LNAME&
&STREET&
&CITY&, &STATE& &ZIP&

Dear &FNAME&:

Thank you for applying for a seat on ESCAPE's first space flight.

Enclosed  you will find all the necessary documents  required  by
Space-Warp  Airways  and the International Aerospace  Consortium.
These forms must be completed and returned by January 1, 1984, in
order for you to be eligible for consideration. Be sure to follow
the instructions outlined in the attached 350-page guide.

In particular,  please be sure your personal therapist  completes
the  orange  psychological-profile form,  listing all  known  and
suspected neuroses, psychoses, and possible paranoid fantasies.

Also be sure that all your former employers,  family members, and
friends  complete  the attached compatibility  questionnaires  to
ensure  that all 15 of our passengers are capable of creating and
sustaining  a  pleasant  and productive  environment  during  our
travel through time and space.

ESCAPE looks forward to welcoming you aboard our first flight  to
the stars.

                                   Sincerely,


                                   Spock Rogers
                                   Quality Control Specialist

Enclosure

.PA
```

HOW TO USE A DATA FILE TO CUSTOMIZE FORM LETTERS

WordStar Comments and Important Notes	*You Enter . . .*
20 WordStar asks: NAME OF FILE TO EDIT? WordStar will transport you to the edit mode. You are now going to design your envelope format.	ENVELOPE.FMT (Press RETURN.)
21 Position the cursor in column 1 of line 1.	(Use cursor-movement commands as necessary.)
22 Now tell WordStar to set a top margin of 12 blank lines (to space down to print the address) and a page length of 24 lines.	.MT 12 (Press RETURN.) .PL 24 (Press RETURN.)
23 Give the command to omit page numbering.	.OP (Press RETURN.)
24 Now tell WordStar the name of the data file you want it to use.	.DF NAMES.LST (Press RETURN.)
25 Next tell WordStar the order of the values it will find in this file. Use three command lines if necessary.	.RV FNAME,LNAME, (Press RETURN.) .RV STREET, (Press RETURN.) .RV CITY,STATE,ZIP (Press RETURN.)

HOW TO USE A DATA FILE TO CUSTOMIZE FORM LETTERS

You Enter . . .	*WordStar Comments and Important Notes*	
(Press RETURN as necessary.)	Now move the cursor down until there is one blank line between the cursor and the last command line.	26
^ I (Six times.)	Tab over to column 31.	27
&FNAME& &LNAME& (Press RETURN.)	Enter the format for the first and last name.	28
^ I (Six times.)	Tab over to column 31 again.	29
&STREET& (Press RETURN.)	Enter the format for the street address.	30
^ I (Six times.)	Tab over to column 31.	31
&CITY&, &STATE& &ZIP& (Press RETURN.)	Enter the format for city, state, and zip code.	32
.PA (Press RETURN.)	Enter a page-break command.	33

HOW TO USE A DATA FILE TO CUSTOMIZE FORM LETTERS

	WordStar Comments and Important Notes	***You Enter . . .***
34	Your envelope format should look like the one below.	(Compare formats.)
35	If it looks good, save this file.	^ KD
36	Now you are ready to print the letters. When the no-file menu reappears on the screen, prepare your printer. Be sure to use continuous-form paper.	(Turn on printer. Insert and align paper.)
37	Tell WordStar you want to merge-print a file.	M

```
.MT 12
.PL 24
.OP
.DF NAMES.LST
.RV FNAME,LNAME,
.RV STREET,
.RV CITY,STATE,ZIP
                                    &FNAME& &LNAME&
                                    &STREET&
                                    &CITY&, &STATE& &ZIP&

.PA
```

HOW TO USE A DATA FILE TO CUSTOMIZE FORM LETTERS

You Enter . . .	*WordStar Comments and Important Notes*	
DFINQRY.LTR (Press ESC.)	WordStar asks: NAME OF FILE TO MERGE-PRINT? WordStar flashes P=STOP PRINT, then prints your letter, filling in the appropriate information where indicated in the file.	**38**
(Press space bar.)	After it has printed all three letters, WordStar asks you to press the space bar to return to the no-file menu.	**39**
(Remove paper. Insert envelope.)	When the no-file menu reappears on the screen, remove the continuous-form paper and insert an envelope.	**40**
M	Tell WordStar you want to merge-print another file.	**41**
ENVELOPE.FMT (Press RETURN.)	WordStar asks: NAME OF FILE TO MERGE-PRINT?	**42**
(Press RETURN.)	WordStar asks: DISK FILE OUTPUT	**43**

HOW TO USE A DATA FILE TO CUSTOMIZE FORM LETTERS

WordStar Comments and Important Notes	*You Enter . . .*
44 WordStar asks: START AT PAGE NUMBER	(Press RETURN.)
45 WordStar asks: STOP AFTER PAGE NUMBER	(Press RETURN.)
46 WordStar asks: NUMBER OF COPIES	(Press RETURN.)
47 WordStar asks: USE FORM FEEDS	(Press RETURN.)
48 WordStar asks: SUPPRESS PAGE FORMATTING	(Press RETURN.)
49 WordStar asks: PAUSE FOR PAPER CHANGE BETWEEN PAGES	Y (Press RETURN.)
50 WordStar advises: Ready printer, press RETURN WordStar flashes P=STOP PRINT, then prints the first envelope.	(Press RETURN.)

HOW TO USE A DATA FILE TO CUSTOMIZE FORM LETTERS

You Enter . . .	*WordStar Comments and Important Notes*	
(Remove envelope. Insert next envelope.) P	When WordStar pauses, you need to remove the printed envelope, put in a fresh one, and tell WordStar to continue printing.	**51**
(Remove envelope. Insert next envelope.) P	WordStar prints the next envelope, then pauses for you to feed in another one.	**52**
(Press space bar.)	WordStar prints the last envelope, then instructs you to press the space bar to return to the no-file menu.	**53**

WHAT YOU JUST DID

You have just discovered how easy it is to create an all-purpose data file that can be used to print many different form letters with matching envelopes. As you can see, this is definitely the preferred method of generating lots of form letters if you have to do quite a lot of them at one time.

All you have to do is:

1. Create a data file of names and addresses and save it.
2. Create a form letter, beginning with the command .OP to omit page numbering. On the next line, enter .DF and the name of your data file. On the next line, enter .RV and the titles, in order, that make up each record in your data file.
3. Type the form letter, inserting &TITLE& codes wherever you want the corresponding values from your data file to appear.
4. End the letter with the page-break command .PA and save the file.
5. Create an envelope-format file, setting a top margin of 12 lines with .MT 12 and a page length of 24 lines with .PL 24. Enter .OP to omit page numbering.
6. Tell WordStar where to find the names and addresses using .DF followed by your data file name, and the order it will find them in using .RV followed by the variable titles.
7. Format the &TITLE& codes as you want them to appear printed on the envelope.
8. Use command M, the form letter file name, and, if using continuous-form paper, press ESCAPE.
9. Use command M and the letter-format file name to print the envelopes, feeding them in one by one. Don't forget to tell WordStar to stop between pages, so you can insert the next envelope.

3
%
^ 6
& 7
* 8
E
Y
S
D
F
H
J
C
V
B
N

twenty-one

MailMerge and Boilerplate Paragraphs

WHEN TO USE MAILMERGE WITH BOILERPLATE PARAGRAPHS

As discussed in section *Eight,* there are advantages to using WordStar commands to create letters with boilerplate paragraphs and there are also advantages to using MailMerge commands. If you use WordStar to read in copies of boilerplate paragraphs, you have the opportunity to edit them as much as necessary to make them really personal. However, you also use up valuable storage space by making duplicate copies of the same paragraph in many different files. When you enter MailMerge commands to read in copies of boilerplate paragraphs, only the command becomes part of the file. The paragraphs themselves are incorporated into the document when it is merge-printed. So when you use MailMerge, you gain storage space but pass up the opportunity to make changes to the paragraph.

That does not mean that you cannot add material between boilerplate paragraphs—you can. For those occasions when you want to add a few words, you can include additional text within a letter that is mostly built of .FI commands. We will show you how in the last part of this exercise.

A good rule of thumb: When boilerplate editing is necessary, use the WordStar skills you learned in section *Eight.* When the boilerplate paragraphs are going to be used as they are, use the MailMerge commands you will learn in this exercise.

WHAT YOU WILL DO

In this exercise, you will use the boilerplate paragraphs you created as files 1 through 8 in section *Eight*. First, you will open a new file and enter the date, inside address, and salutation. Then you will enter MailMerge's file insert command, .FI, to specify the boilerplate paragraphs you want to use. You will save this file, then merge-print it to see how you did. Then you will repeat the whole exercise, this time adding your own paragraph in the middle of the boilerplate paragraphs to produce a customized letter.

HOW TO USE MAILMERGE AND BOILERPLATE PARAGRAPHS FOR LETTERS

	WordStar Comments and Important Notes	***You Enter . . .***
1	When the no-file menu appears on the screen, tell WordStar you want to create a new file.	D
2	WordStar asks: NAME OF FILE TO EDIT? WordStar flashes the message NEW FILE, then transports you to the edit mode.	NEWLTR-1 (Press RETURN.)
3	Enter the text you see on the next page.	(Enter text.)
4	Position the cursor in column 1 of the second blank line below the salutation.	(Use cursor-movement commands as necessary.)

```
                                December 2, 1983


Mr. O. T. Lunch
3 Martini Way
Noe, Texas 18947

Dear Mr. Lunch:
```

You Enter . . .	*WordStar Comments and Important Notes*	
.FI 2 (Press RETURN.)	Now enter the MailMerge command to tell WordStar to read in one of your boilerplate paragraph files. The cursor is now positioned in column 1 of the blank line just below the command you just typed.	**5**
.FI 4 (Press RETURN.)	Enter your next file insert command. The cursor is now positioned in column 1 of the next blank line.	**6**
.FI 7 (Press RETURN.)	Enter the file insert command to add your closing paragraph. Make sure the cursor is positioned in column 1 of the next blank line.	**7**

HOW TO USE MAILMERGE AND BOILERPLATE PARAGRAPHS FOR LETTERS

WordStar Comments and Important Notes	*You Enter . . .*
8 Add the file insert command to add the signature block. Notice that we did not tell you to include blank lines between each .FI command. You do not have to, because you included one blank line at the end of each boilerplate paragraph you stored. When you use the .FI command, the whole contents of the specified file are inserted in your document, including any blank lines (or carriage returns) at the beginning and end of the file. If you discover that your paragraphs end up all jammed together, you have two choices: You can go back and add a blank line to the end of each boilerplate paragraph, or you can double-space between .FI commands when you enter them, so that WordStar knows to put a blank line between the paragraphs when it inserts them.	.FI 8 (Press RETURN.)
9 Complete this letter by adding the omit-page-number command.	.OP (Press RETURN.)
10 Your screen should look like the one at the top of the next page.	(Compare texts.)

```
                    December 2, 1983


Mr. O. T. Lunch
3 Martini Way
Noe, Texas 18947

Dear Mr. Lunch:

.FI 2
.FI 4
.FI 7
.FI 8
.OP
```

You Enter . . .	***WordStar Comments and Important Notes***	
^ KD	If your copy looks just like ours, save this file.	**11**
(Turn on printer. Insert paper.)	When the no-file menu reappears on the screen, prepare your printer.	**12**
M	Tell WordStar you want to merge-print a file.	**13**
NEWLTR-1 (Press ESC.)	WordStar asks: NAME OF FILE TO MERGE-PRINT? WordStar prints your letter, pasting in the paragraphs you specified as it goes along.	**14**

HOW TO USE MAILMERGE AND BOILERPLATE PARAGRAPHS FOR LETTERS

WordStar Comments and Important Notes	*You Enter . . .*
15 This is what your finished letter should look like:	(Compare letters.)

December 2, 1983

Mr. O. T. Lunch
3 Martini Way
Noe, Texas 18947

Dear Mr. Lunch:

We regret to advise that we will be unable to reserve a seat for you on our first flight aboard the USS Orwell.

Unfortunately, the report received from your therapist indicated that you have experienced, or will experience significant psychological trauma that might make it unwise for you to participate in space travel.

We will be happy to reconsider your application if you can provide additional material proving the above claims untrue. Simply complete the enclosed 14 forms and attach a check for $1,000 to cover reprocessing costs.

Sincerely,

Spock Rogers
Quality Control Specialist

WHAT YOU JUST DID

You have just created a letter by mixing and matching boilerplate paragraphs without having to take up disk space by copying them. This is how you did it:

1. Create a numbered list of boilerplate paragraphs and save it as a master file.
2. Save each paragraph followed by a blank line in its own file.
3. Open a new file and enter the date, address, and salutation.
4. Use MailMerge's file insert command, .FI, followed by the file name of the paragraph you want WordStar to print next. Use .FI as often as you need.
5. Save this file and then merge-print it.

Now isn't that faster than reading in those paragraphs? Of course, you do have to know the name and contents of your boilerplate paragraphs, or you may be surprised by what WordStar types in. That is why it is a good idea to keep a master list of your paragraphs for reference.

Now we will show you how to add new material to a letter that includes .FI commands.

HOW TO ADD TO A MAILMERGE/BOILERPLATE PARAGRAPH LETTER

	WordStar Comments and Important Notes	*You Enter . . .*
1	When the no-file menu appears on the screen, tell WordStar you want to create or edit a file.	D
2	WordStar asks: NAME OF FILE TO EDIT? WordStar briefly flashes the message NEW FILE, then transports you to the edit mode.	NEWLTR-2 (Press RETURN.)
3	Enter the text you see opposite. Be sure to enter each dot command on a line by itself, with the period entered in column 1. End each command by pressing RETURN.	(Enter text.)
4	Review your letter to make sure it looks just like ours. If it is correct, save it.	^ KD

```
                         April 1, 1984


Mr. Haus Tillman
86 Grough Way
Ruff and Ready, CA 93894

Dear Mr. Tillman:

.FI 2
.FI 5

As a matter of fact,  due to the reports we received (and some of
them  were  quite detailed),  we think it unlikely that we  could
ever consider you for passage aboard an ESCAPE flight.  Have  you
considered Alaska?

.FI 8
.OP
```

You Enter . . .	*WordStar Comments and Important Notes*	
(Turn on printer. Insert paper.)	When the no-file menu reappears on the screen, prepare your printer.	**5**
M	Tell WordStar you are ready to merge-print a file.	**6**
NEWLTR-2 (Press ESC.)	WordStar asks: NAME OF FILE TO MERGE-PRINT? WordStar prints your letter, inserting the boilerplate paragraphs where specified by the .FI commands.	**7**
(Compare letters.)	Your printed letter should look like the one on the next page.	**8**

```
                              April 1, 1984


Mr. Haus Tillman
86 Grough Way
Ruff and Ready, CA 93894

Dear Mr. Tillman:

We  regret to advise that we will be unable to reserve a seat for
you on our first flight aboard the USS Orwell.

Unfortunately,  the  questionnaires completed by your  employers,
family members, and friends indicated that it is not possible for
you to maintain civil relations with most of the people with whom
you come in contact on a regular basis.

As a matter of fact,  due to the reports we received (and some of
them  were quite detailed),  we think it unlikely that  we  could
ever  consider you for passage aboard an ESCAPE flight.  Have you
considered Alaska?

                              Sincerely,



                              Spock Rogers
                              Quality Control Specialist
```

WHAT YOU JUST DID

Congratulations! You have just completed the last of the exercises in this book. In this last one, you polished your understanding of MailMerge's boilerplate capability. As you discovered, it is easy to mix your own words with standard paragraphs that fit most situations.

Notice that you began your own paragraph on the line immediately following a .FI command, because there is a blank line included at the end of each boilerplate paragraph file. However, you did have to add a blank line between your paragraph and the .FI command that followed it, because you had not stored a blank line at the beginning of your boilerplate paragraph files.

#
3
%
^
6
&
7
*
8
E
Y
S
D
F
H
J
C
V
B
N

Where Do You Go from Here?

If you have successfully completed the exercises in this book, you are a qualified WordStar operator. Congratulations! You now have the skills necessary to use the full power of WordStar to produce many complex applications with very little effort. That is the whole purpose of word processing—to make the mechanical process of producing a printed document as easy as possible. And now you know how!

So where do you go from here? You are probably qualified to begin training other people to use WordStar productively. If you liked the format of our instructions, feel free to record your applications using the same format, so that you can use them in conjunction with our book to train your friends and co-workers.

If you feel that you have just begun to scratch the surface of automated office processing, you might be interested in reviewing *Appendix D,* which is an overview of other programs that can be used in cooperation with WordStar to enhance its capabilities. If you already own InfoStar, MicroPro's new report program, watch for a forthcoming Sybex book, by Julie Anne Arca and Charles Pirro. It provides the same application-oriented instruction for InfoStar that was used in this book for WordStar.

If you think you are not ready to conquer another program just yet, don't feel bad about taking the time to explore WordStar further. It is such a powerful program that it can take years to discover all its little tricks and techniques. Start by saying *I wonder what would happen if I tried this . . .* Then try it!

appendix a

WordStar Commands at a Glance

As you know, WordStar offers many different ways to word process. Because it is so flexible, it can seem overwhelming to a beginner. To help overcome this, we have put together a list of 22 WordStar commands that can see you through your first attempts at entering, editing, and formatting text.

As you learn more about WordStar, you will find other commands to enhance those listed. However, you can do just about anything you need with these commands, so while you are still a novice, concentrate on learning just this list.

WHEN YOU ARE IN . . .	IN ORDER TO . . .	YOU ENTER . . .
Operating system	Begin using WordStar	WS (Press RETURN)
No-file menu	Create or edit a file	D
	Print a document	P
Edit-mode main menu	Move cursor left one character	^ S
	Move cursor right one character	^ D
	Move cursor up one line	^ E
	Move cursor down one line	^ X
	Move screen display one page closer to beginning of document	^ R
	Move screen display one page closer to end of document	^ C
	Move screen display to beginning of document	^ QR
	Move screen display to end of document	^ QC
	Delete character covered by cursor	^ G
	Delete line on which cursor is positioned	^ Y
	Insert text at cursor location (if INSERT OFF)	^ V
	Reformat paragraph after making changes	^ B
	Change left margin setting	^ OL
	Change right margin setting	^ OR
	Center line of text on which cursor is positioned	^ OC
	Save completed document on disk	^ KD
	Get help!	^ J
	Omit page numbering	.OP
	End one page and begin a new one	.PA

appendix b
More Help with CP/M

In section *One,* you learned how to boot the system, change the logged disk drive, and reset the computer system. You also learned how to create acceptable file names.

In this *Appendix,* we remind you how to perform the most basic CP/M file-handling functions, including running a program, listing the names of files stored on a disk, copying files, erasing files, renaming files, and determining the storage capacity of a disk.

HOW TO RUN A PROGRAM

As you know, the addition of the file-type designator .COM to a file name indicates to CP/M that a particular file is a program. For example, the WordStar program file is called WS.COM. To use a program file, you tell CP/M to run (start) it by simply typing the program file name and pressing RETURN. You do not need to type the file-type designator .COM—CP/M will check the directory to make sure the file ends with .COM.

For example, to run the WordStar program, type:

WS (Press RETURN.)

CP/M will turn over control of your computer to WordStar.

When typing a program file name, CP/M does not care if you use upper- or lowercase characters. Just make sure you spell the name the same way it appears in the directory.

WHICH FILES ARE STORED ON THIS DISK?

If you are a conscientious operator, you are probably careful to put a label on each disk you use, listing the files that are stored on that disk. However, it is a good idea to confirm that you have inserted the correct disk by asking CP/M to list the names of the files stored on the disk.

Checking the Directory of the Logged Disk Drive

To display the directory of files stored on the disk inserted in the logged disk drive, type:

DIR (Press RETURN.)

CP/M will display a list of the names of all the files stored on that disk.

Checking the Directory of an Unlogged Disk Drive

To display a list of the files stored on a disk inserted in an unlogged disk drive, use the same DIR command followed by the appropriate drive letter or number and a colon. For example, to see the names of the files stored on drive B, type:

DIR B: (Press RETURN.)

CP/M will take a look at your unlogged disk drive and display a list of the files stored on it.

Freezing a Moving Directory Listing

If your system displays the file directory in columns across the video screen, it should be possible for you to view the whole directory at once.

On the other hand, if your system displays the file names in a single column running down the left side of your video screen and you have a lot of files stored on the disk, you will have a hard time reading all the names as they run by on the screen.

If this is the case, use the command ^S (remember, hold down the control key and press S) to stop the listing. Once you have read all the file names displayed on the screen, enter the command ^S again to continue. You can use this command as often as necessary to stop and start the directory display.

HOW TO COPY FILES

As a smart word-processing operator, you will frequently make a copy of important document files on a carefully stored archive disk. When the active data disk that you use regularly finally wears out (or dies prematurely due to accidental abuse), you will be able to recover those irreplaceable files by pulling your archive disk out of storage.

Every disk operating system includes a program to copy files from one disk to another. In CP/M, the program is called PIP (for Peripheral Interchange Program) and is listed on your system disk as PIP.COM, with the .COM file designator indicating that it is a program. As with all program files, PIP.COM must be stored on one of the disks inserted in your drives in order for you to use it. You will remember that, in section *Two,* we suggested that you copy PIP.COM onto your working WordStar disk so that you can copy files you have produced with WordStar.

To copy a file, first type PIP. Then tell CP/M which disk you want to copy to by typing the drive letter or number followed by a colon, which disk you are copying from by typing = followed by the drive letter or number and a colon, and the name(s) of the file(s) you want to copy. Finally, add the command [V] to tell CP/M to verify that the copies match the originals. Do not forget to press RETURN, to tell CP/M to begin operation.

For example, we can use the PIP program to copy itself to another disk by entering:

PIP B: = A:PIP.COM[V] (Press RETURN.)

This command means copy (PIP) to drive B (B:) from (=) drive A (A:) the file named PIP.COM (PIP.COM) and verify that the copy just made matches the original ([V]).

Notice that we run the program by just typing PIP, but that we must type its whole name, PIP.COM, to identify the program file when we want to copy it.

We have assumed that you are currently logged on to your working WordStar program disk, which includes the program file called PIP.COM. If you happened to be logged on to a data disk in drive B, you would follow the same sequence, but precede the copy command with the correct drive designation so that CP/M would know where to find the program. For example, to copy a file when you are logged on to drive B, enter:

A:PIP B: = A:PIP.COM[V] (Press RETURN.)

Copying More than One File at a Time

If you want to copy all the program files (which all have the file-type designator .COM) from one disk to another, use the CP/M wild-card feature to copy them all with one command. Assuming that you want to copy from drive B to drive A, type:

PIP A: = B:*.COM[V] (Press RETURN.)

While it is copying the files, CP/M will list their exact names. When it has finished copying, it will display the A prompt.

Precautions while Copying

Remember, the copy command sequence is *to* one disk *from* another disk. If you are not careful to use this precise sequence, you may find yourself copying the wrong files.

Make sure that you are not copying a file onto a disk that already holds a file with the same name. If PIP finds a file on the destination disk that has the same name as a file it has been told to copy, it will copy the new file over the already existing file of the same name. In other words, the new file will *replace* the existing file.

HOW TO ERASE FILES

From time to time, you may want to erase a file from a disk. It is good to get in the habit of cleaning house regularly by deleting files you never want to use again. That way, you avoid running out of disk space just when you need to store an important file. Besides, if you leave a lot of miscellaneous, useless files on a disk, you will find it increasingly difficult to sort through them to find the names of files you need.

To erase a file, enter the command ERA, a space, and the file name and press RETURN. The prompt will disappear for a second. When it reappears on your screen, check your file directory to make sure that the name of the erased file has been removed from the listing.

Erasing More than One File at a Time

You may use the CP/M wild-card symbol * to erase selected types of files. Enter the erase command and a file name that incorporates the wild-card symbol. For example, to erase all WordStar-generated backup copies, enter:

ERA *.BAK (Press RETURN.)

Just be sure you really want to erase all those files all before you press RETURN and send the command to CP/M.

Precautions while Erasing

Be very careful when you use this command. CP/M does not ask you to confirm your decision before it erases a file. Once a file is erased, it is next to impossible to recover it, unless you have bought a special program that can reconstruct erased files.

Make it a habit to type the ERA command, pause to reread the entry to make sure you typed the right file name, and then press RETURN to send the command to CP/M.

HOW TO RENAME FILES

If you decide that a file name is inappropriate, or if you think of a better one, you may want to rename a file. You may also want to save a WordStar .BAK file by renaming it so it is removed from the automatic updating and deletion process.

To rename a file, you must type the renaming command REN, the new name of the file, the equals sign =, and then the old (current) name of the file. Press RETURN to tell CP/M to begin operation. For example, entering:

REN NEWFILE = OLDFILE (Press RETURN.)

will cause the file named OLDFILE to be renamed NEWFILE.

You will know the file name has been changed if the prompt disappears for a second and then reappears. Check the directory to confirm that the new name has relaced the old in the listing.

Precautions while Renaming

If the prompt disappears for a second and then reappears with the comment NOT FOUND, you made one of two errors: You may have misspelled the old file name, so that CP/M could not find it in the directory; or you may have entered the old name to the left of the equal sign, and the new name to the right. When CP/M looked for the new file name in the directory, it could not find it.

If you made a mistake or want to rename the file again, just re-enter the appropriate command sequence. You may rename files as often as you want. In case you are wondering, you cannot use the CP/M wild-card symbol to change a whole group of file names at once. CP/M requires that you rename files individually.

HOW MUCH SPACE IS LEFT ON THIS DISK?

It is very important to make sure that there is enough space left on the disk to store any new files you may create using WordStar. If you attempt to store a WordStar file on a disk that is already full, WordStar will advise you that there is no space left and force you to abandon the file. You can avoid this problem by always checking space availability before you leave CP/M and enter WordStar to begin word processing.

There is a CP/M status program that can be used to determine the available storage capacity of a disk. Appropriately, it is called STAT.COM. As with PIP.COM, in order to use STAT.COM, it must be stored on one of the disks inserted in your drives. You will remember that, in section *Two,* we suggested that you copy STAT.COM onto your working WordStar disk so that you can check space availability on your WordStar disks.

You can find out how much space is left on the disk by entering:

STAT (Press RETURN.)

We have assumed that you are currently logged on to your working WordStar program disk, which includes the program file called STAT.COM. If you happened to be logged on to a data disk in drive B, you would follow the same sequence, but would precede the STAT command with the correct drive designation, so CP/M would know where to find the program. For example, to check the capacity of your disks when you are logged on to drive B, enter:

A:STAT (Press RETURN.)

If you have disks in both drives, STAT may respond with something like this:

A: R/W, SPACE: 250K
B: R/W, SPACE: 320K

The available storage capacity is reported in number of K (kilobytes), each K being a thousand characters. The STAT program also tells you whether the disk is a read/write (R/W) disk or a read only (R/O) disk. The files on a read/write disk can be displayed and edited, and the revised versions of the files stored on the disk. The files on a read only disk can be displayed, copied, or printed but you cannot make any changes to them.

You can decide whether a disk will be designated R/W or R/O. In most cases, all you have to do is cover or expose a notch cut into the side of the floppy disk.

appendix c

BASIC IBM PC-DOS Operations

Before you read this *Appendix,* you might want to read the introduction to section *One: Getting Past the Disk Operating System,* so you understand the importance of a computer's operating system. In many ways IBM PC-DOS is very similar to the CP/M operating system. In this *Appendix,* we will show you how to boot the system, switch between logged drives, and use some basic PC-DOS commands.

WAKING UP YOUR COMPUTER

Waking up your computer means inserting a system disk in a disk drive, turning your PC on, and preparing the computer to start accepting commands from you. This is known as booting the system.

Your IBM PC will always check the same drive each time it is turned on. This drive, the one on the left side, is the one into which you must insert the system disk (the one that has PC-DOS on it). PC-DOS calls this drive *A*, even though the drive is not actually labeled A.

When you have successfully awakened your IBM PC, you will see this message:

```
Current date is (last date entered)
Enter new date:_
```

You enter the date by typing a one- or two-digit number for the month, a one- or two-digit number for the day, and a two- or four-digit number for the year, in that order. You can separate the numbers with either hyphens or slashes, but you must leave no spaces within the date. For example, you might enter 12-29-83 or 2/4/1984. Complete the date entry by pressing RETURN (the key with the broken left arrow).

You do not have to enter a date; when the IBM PC asks you to enter the new date, you can just press RETURN. After you press RETURN, the following message will be displayed:

```
Current time is (last time entered)
Enter new time:_
```

Enter the time by typing a one- or two-digit number for the hour, a one- or two-digit number for the minutes, a one- or two-digit number for the seconds, and a one- or two-digit number for hundredths of seconds. (Hundredths of seconds are optional.)

Type a colon between the hours and the minutes and between the minutes and seconds, but type a period between the seconds and hundredths of seconds. Leave no spaces within the time. For example, 4:26:42.08 or 7:03:59. Complete the entry by pressing RETURN.

If you do not want to enter the time, you can just press RETURN when the IBM PC asks you to enter a new time. After you press

RETURN, you will see *A>* displayed on your video screen. This is PC-DOS's way of saying *Hello, you are using disk drive A. What do you want to do?* This announcement is known as the A prompt, because you are being prompted by your computer to give a command.

MOVING AROUND THE DISK OPERATING SYSTEM

As we have said, your computer always accesses drive A first. If you have two disk drives, you might want to insert a disk into each drive, so that you can access more than one disk of information while you are working. For example, it is sometimes helpful to use a disk that contains only the operating system and the WordStar programs in drive A. You can then insert a data disk in drive B to store the documents you create with WordStar. Because data disks are not cluttered up with the PC-DOS or WordStar programs, you will be able to store many more pages of text on each disk.

Choosing the Right Drive

If you insert disks in both drives A and B, you probably will want to be able to look directly at the information you have stored on the disk inserted in drive B. To do this, you must log on to that disk. Logging on means telling the operating system to direct its attention to a specific disk drive. As you know, PC-DOS automatically logs on to drive A when you first turn on your computer. You can then log on to another drive with the appropriate PC-DOS command.

Access the information stored on the disk in drive B by typing *B:* and pressing RETURN. Notice that the PC-DOS prompt now displays *B>* to indicate that you have successfully logged on to drive B. Any commands you give PC-DOS while B> is displayed will be executed on files stored on the disk inserted in drive B.

Any time you want to switch between disk drives, enter the drive letter you want and a colon and then press RETURN. The appropriately lettered prompt will be displayed on your video screen, and you will be able to execute commands on files stored on the disk in the indicated drive.

Changing Disks

What if you discover that you are working with the wrong disk? What if you use all the available space on a disk? Well, you can remove the disk, turn off the computer, and start over—but there is an easier way.

After removing a disk from any drive and inserting a new one, press simultaneously the Ctrl and Alt keys on the left of the keyboard and the Del key on the right. This built-in PC-DOS command acts as a reset switch. It clears out anything currently stored in the internal working memory of your computer (RAM) and takes a fresh look at the disks stored in the drive. When the prompt reappears, you will know that PC-DOS is starting from scratch, as if you had just turned on your computer for the first time.

ASSIGNING PC-DOS FILE NAMES

The first thing you do when you set up a manual filing system is assign names to each of the files you want to store. To make sure your file clerk can quickly store and retrieve the files, you must be very careful to assign names that follow a standard format.

Every document you create with WordStar is also a file. Your computer's file clerk (PC-DOS) requires that you assign a name to each computerized file you create. To make sure PC-DOS can quickly locate any files you have stored on disk, a few important rules have been established for developing file names. You must abide by these conventions. If you don't, PC-DOS will be unable to access information stored on your disk.

The rules for creating PC-DOS (and WordStar) file names are:

1. All PC-DOS file names consist of a maximum of eight contiguous characters. If you try to use more than eight, PC-DOS will ignore anything past the eighth one. You may use less than eight characters.

2. These characters may be letters (upper- or lowercase), numbers, or some punctation marks. You cannot use the asterisk (*) or the question mark (?) as part of a file name because PC-DOS uses these symbols as special codes, nor can you use any of the following: < > . , : ; = [ ] .

3. Do not include any spaces between characters.

As you have probably realized, there are only so many creative ways to use eight characters in a file name and still have a reasonable chance of guessing what is in the file. To give you more flexibility, PC-DOS and WordStar allow you to add a file type at the end of the eight-character file name so you can key different types of files. Naturally, there are rules for the development of these file types, too.

1. You may add a period and a maximum of three additional characters to a file name to code different types of files. For example, you might use the file type .MSS to define manuscripts, .LTR to define letters, and .FRM to define forms.
2. Do not use the file type .COM. This is reserved by PC-DOS to indicate that a file is a command file, a program (list of instructions) that tells the computer how to perform specific functions or applications. For example, the WordStar program is usually coded WS.COM to let PC-DOS know that it is a program, not a document file.
3. Do not use the file type .BAK, either. WordStar uses this file type to code backup versions of files that it automatically creates every time you reedit a file. Other file types you cannot use are .OVR, .ASM, and .PRN.
4. Do not include any spaces within the file type or between the file name and the file type. You may use any upper- or lowercase letters, numbers, or any character except the asterisk and the question mark in the file type.

USING PC-DOS'S WILD-CARD SYMBOLS

If you develop and consistently use standard file names, you can instruct PC-DOS to perform many file-handling operations on whole groups of specified file types. This is where the wild-card symbols, the asterisk and the question mark, flex their muscles. After you have typed a PC-DOS command, you may use the * or the ? within a file name to indicate that you wish to perform that function on all files having certain characteristics.

The * Wild Card

The asterisk is used to indicate that you want to perform a function on all files that include certain characters. For example, you may want a directory of only your program files. Although the file names are all different, you know that all program files end with the file type .COM, so you type the PC-DOS directory command followed by *.COM. PC-DOS displays only those file names ending in .COM, such as WS.COM. Use the * wild card whenever there are many similar files you want to perform certain functions on. The asterisk signifies *any character or characters.*

The ? Wild Card

The question-mark wild card is useful when you have a few files whose names are exactly the same except for one character that appears in the same position in them all. For example, if you wanted a listing of all your Jones letters, you might type the file name JONES?.LTR to list files names JONES1.LTR, JONES2.LTR, and JONES3.LTR. However, using the question mark as a wild card, PC-DOS would not list JONES10.LTR, because you told it to list only those files where the first five characters were JONES, there was any character in position six, and the sixth character was immediately followed by the file type .LTR.

You can use these wild card symbols in conjunction with most PC-DOS commands to save time managing your disk file system.

HOW TO RUN A PROGRAM

As mentioned above, the addition of the file type designator .COM to a file name indicates to PC-DOS that a particular file is a program. For example, the WordStar program file is called WS.COM. To use a program file, tell PC-DOS to run it by typing the program file name and pressing RETURN. Don't type the file type designator .COM.

For example, to run the WordStar program, all you have to do is type WS and press RETURN. PC-DOS will turn over control of your computer to WordStar.

WHICH FILES ARE STORED ON THIS DISK?

If you are a conscientious operator you are probably careful to put labels on each disk you use, listing the files that are stored on that disk. However, it is a good idea to confirm that you have actually inserted the correct disk by asking PC-DOS to list the names of the files stored on the disk.

Checking the Directory of the Logged Disk Drive

To display the directory of files stored on the disk inserted in the logged disk drive, type *DIR* and press RETURN. PC-DOS will display a list of the names of all the files stored on that disk.

Checking the Directory of the Unlogged Disk Drive

To display a list of the files stored on a disk inserted in an unlogged disk drive, use the same DIR command followed by the appropriate drive letter and a colon. For example, to see the names of the files stored on drive B, type *DIR B:* and press RETURN. PC-DOS will glance at your second disk drive and display a list of the files stored on it.

HOW TO COPY FILES

As a smart word-processing operator, you will frequently make copies of important document files on an archive disk, which you carefully store away. When the disk you use on a regular basis (the active disk) finally wears out, you will be able to recover those irreplaceable files by pulling out your archive disks.

Every operating system includes a program to copy files from one disk to another. With PC-DOS, the command to use this program is COPY.

Copying a File from One Disk to Another

To copy a file, first type COPY, then the name of the file you want to copy and the drive letter to which it should be copied. Don't forget to press RETURN to tell PC-DOS to begin operation.

For example, we can use the COPY command to copy WS.COM to another disk. You would type COPY WS.COM B:, and press RETURN. This command means copy the file named WS.COM onto the disk inserted in drive B.

Copying More than One File at a Time

If you want to copy all of the program (.COM) files from one disk to another, use the PC-DOS * wild card to copy all of them with one command. Let's assume that you want to copy from drive B to drive A. You would type COPY B:*.COM A: and press RETURN. When it has finished copying, PC-DOS will tell you how many files it copied, then display the A prompt.

HOW TO ERASE FILES

From time to time, you may want to erase a file stored on a disk. It is a good idea to clean house on a regular basis by deleting files you never want to use again. That way, you will avoid running out of disk space when you attempt to store an important file. Besides, if you leave a lot of miscellaneous and useless files on a disk, you will find it increasingly difficult to sort through them to find the names of the files you do need.

To erase a file, type the command ERASE followed by the file name and press RETURN. The prompt will disappear for a second and will then reappear on your screen. After the prompt reappears, you can check your file directory to make sure that the name of the erased file has been removed from the listing.

Erasing More than One File at a Time

You may use the PC-DOS wild-card symbol * to erase selected types of files. Enter the erase command and a file name that incorporates the wild-card symbol. For example, to erase all WordStar generated backup copies, type ERASE *.BAK, and press RETURN. Just be sure you really want to erase all those files before you press RETURN and send the command to PC-DOS.

Precautions while Erasing

Be very careful when you use this command. PC-DOS does not ask you to confirm your decision before it erases a file. Once a file is erased, it is next to impossible to recover it, unless you buy a special program that can reconstruct the file.

Make it a habit to type the ERASE command, pause to reread the entry to make sure you typed the right file name, and then press RETURN to send the command to PC-DOS.

HOW TO RENAME FILES

If you decide that a file name is inappropriate, or if you think of a better one, you may want to rename a file. You may also want to save a WordStar .BAK file by renaming it so it is removed from the automatic updating and deletion process.

To rename a file, you type the RENAME command, the present name of the file, then the new name of the file. Don't forget to press RETURN to tell PC-DOS to begin operation. For example, if you type RENAME OLDNAME NEWNAME and press RETURN, the file named OLDNAME will be renamed NEWNAME.

You know the file name has been changed if the prompt disappears for a second and then reappears. Check the directory to confirm that the new name has replaced the old.

Precautions while Renaming

If the prompt disappears for a second and then reappears with the comment FILE NOT FOUND, you made one of two errors: You may have misspelled the old file name, so that PC-DOS could not find it; or you may have entered the new name first and then the old name. When PC-DOS looked for the new file name, it couldn't find it.

If you made a mistake or want to rename the file, just re-enter the appropriate command sequence. You may rename files as often as you want. In case you are wondering, you cannot use the PC-DOS wild-card symbols to change a whole group of file names at a time. PC-DOS requires that you rename files one at a time.

HOW MUCH SPACE IS LEFT ON THIS DISK?

It is very important to make sure that there is enough space left on the disk to store any new files you may create using WordStar. If you attempt to store a WordStar file on a disk that is already full, WordStar will advise you that there is no space left and force you to abandon the file. You can avoid this problem by always checking space availability before you leave PC-DOS and enter WordStar to begin word processing.

PC-DOS has a program that you can use to determine the available storage capacity of a disk. Appropriately, it is called CHKDSK.COM. Because it is a program, CHKDSK.COM must be stored on the disk inserted in the logged drive in order for you to use it. In other words, the file name CHKDSK.COM must appear in the disk directory when you type DIR.

You can find out how much space is left on the disk by typing CHKDSK and pressing RETURN. The program will check your disk and respond with something like this:

```
160257 bytes total disk space

  8195 bytes in 2 hidden files
  5605 bytes in 4 user files
  3096 bytes in bad sectors
143365 bytes available on disk

 65336 bytes total memory
 53104 bytes free
```

PC-DOS reports both the amount of disk storage available and the amount of internal working memory (RAM) available in numbers of bytes. A byte is the amount of space needed to store a character—a letter, number, or punctuation mark.

If you figure that it takes about 3,000 characters (bytes) to store one page of text on a disk, according to the above report, you have space to store about 47 more pages on this disk.

Hidden files are PC-DOS files that do not appear when you use the command DIR. They are part of the internal workings of the operating system that you do not need to worry about—except when you are calculating whether you have enough space left to store a document. That is why these hidden files are included in the CHKDSK report.

appendix d

Enhancing the Power of WordStar

WordStar is a powerful word-processing program that provides most of the editing and print-formatting features required by anyone who writes anything. However, by itself, it is not the answer to every word-processing problem encountered in the home or office.

In this *Appendix,* we will briefly review programs published by MicroPro, the distributor of WordStar, that were designed to enhance the power of WordStar. We will also mention some of the enhancement programs produced by other companies, which can be used in conjunction with WordStar to provide complete control of the written word.

SPELLSTAR

SpellStar is one of the optional programs listed in WordStar's no-file menu. If you own the SpellStar program, and if it is stored on the disk inserted in the logged disk drive, you may access it from within WordStar. It does not matter if SpellStar is stored on your working WordStar disk or your data disk, but you must log on to the drive on which SpellStar is stored before you can access the program. Once accessed, you may use SpellStar to proofread any of the documents you have created using WordStar.

Included with the SpellStar program is a dictionary of over 20,000 words. As SpellStar reviews your document, it tries to match each word in the document with a word in its dictionary. If it can find a match, it assumes that the word is correctly spelled. If it cannot find a match, it assumes that the word is misspelled.

Obviously, any names (such as your company name) or technical words peculiar to your industry (such as RAM) are not included in the original dictionary. Until you add these special words, SpellStar always assumes that they are incorrectly spelled.

After proofreading your document, SpellStar lists the number of words in your document and the number of unique words. For example, you may have written a letter of 500 words but have used only 200 different ones, since words like *the, a,* and *that* are usually used more than once in a document.

Next, SpellStar tells you how many words it was unable to match with those in its dictionary, and asks if you want to see a list of the words it thinks are misspelled. If you say yes, SpellStar displays these words on your video screen. If they are all proper nouns or technical words, you may want to abandon SpellStar because there are really no misspelled words. If, on the other hand, you did misspell several words, you can ask SpellStar to mark the errors in the document.

Once it has marked them, you can go back to WordStar's edit mode to correct the errors. SpellStar stays around, however, so that it can point out the possible errors. It will move the cursor to each error and ask whether you want to correct it, ignore it (for example, if it is a name), bypass it for now so you can look it up, or add the word to its dictionary. Once you have reviewed each possible misspelling, you can save the corrected document using any one of WordStar's normal save commands.

As you check each possible misspelling, SpellStar stores all the words you decide to add to its dictionary in a separate file. After correcting your whole document for spelling errors, you can return to SpellStar and direct it to sort the stored words and insert them in its dictionary.

SpellStar is an extremely efficient and useful program. However, like all spelling-checker programs, it does not really read your document or understand its content. It simply matches all the words in your document against all the words in its dictionary. If you typed *there* instead of *their,* SpellStar does not have the brains to realize that you typed the wrong word. It will catch all true misspellings, but you should still have a colleague quickly review the finished document to avoid errors caused by correctly spelling the wrong word.

DATASTAR

DataStar is MicroPro's data-entry program. Using this program, you first create a standard questionnaire format that includes all the information you want to maintain on each customer, client, or item. Then a blank questionnaire is displayed on the video screen, and can be filled in by the operator.

For example, you might create a name and address questionnaire that includes spaces for NAME, STREET ADDRESS, CITY, STATE, ZIP CODE, and TELEPHONE. For each customer, you would fill in all the blanks and then save that information as a record on a disk. One or more such records could make up a data file. Still using DataStar, you can recall any record, edit it, delete it, or print a copy of it.

So where does WordStar fit into this? Well, WordStar cannot talk directly to DataStar, but MailMerge can talk to both. For example, imagine a WordStar form letter that includes MailMerge commands to pull names and addresses from the name and address file that you created with DataStar. MailMerge links the WordStar letter with the DataStar names and addresses, and you end up with a perfectly typed, personalized letter to each of your many customers.

In the MailMerge exercises included in this book, you discovered that it is fairly easy to create a data file with WordStar. However, you only entered three records in the data file. Imagine how difficult it would be to find, edit, or delete one record when it is sandwiched in among 300 other records.

Using WordStar, it would not be unusual for an operator to insert an extra space accidentally or forget a required comma. If that happens, WordStar may insert the wrong information in a document, or be unable to read the information at all. Using DataStar, the operator can ask to view the form that holds that one record, and can easily modify any part of it without risk of making undesirable changes to other parts of that record or any other record.

If you need to create a data file that holds only a few records, use WordStar. If you need to create a data file that holds many records that are edited frequently, use DataStar.

SUPERSORT

MicroPro's SuperSort program has been rated as one of the most sophisticated, efficient, and fast sorting programs in the industry. What does sorting have to do with word processing?

Well, for example, take that list of names and addresses you created using DataStar. What do you do if you just want to send a letter to people in a certain zip code? Neither DataStar nor MailMerge is capable of selecting only certain records from a file—they are all-or-nothing kinds of programs. However, if you use SuperSort to select all the appropriate records and store them in a separate file, you can then use MailMerge to merge these selected names and addresses with a WordStar document.

SuperSort includes commands to sort alphabetically and/or numerically, selecting only those records that include information greater than or less than the criterion you specify. For example, you could sort through a customer file to select only those customers who had spent more than $1,000 in the last year, but had not ordered within the last 90 days, and who lived in a specified range of zip codes.

You can thus use SuperSort to create specialized lists from a massive DataStar file, then use WordStar with MailMerge to create personalized letters to many different segments of your marketplace. How is that for selective marketing!

INFOSTAR

The newest addition to MicroPro's family of software, InfoStar includes DataStar, a version of SuperSort, and a brand new program called ReportStar. DataStar operates as usual—use it to create and fill in a custom-designed questionnaire. The modified version of SuperSort is a little easier to use than the original version, because MicroPro has added some helpful prompting to make sure you set up the sorting criteria properly. ReportStar is the most exciting new part of the package. It allows you to create reports from the DataStar records. It can print columns, add totals, and provide analysis of your information.

Whereas WordStar handles your word-processing needs, InfoStar can handle your information-processing needs by preparing statistical reports. The reports generated by InfoStar can be included in documents created in WordStar.

OTHER COMPATIBLE PROGRAMS

Because WordStar is so popular, many other software companies have developed software that can enhance its word-processing power. Below you will find a very brief overview of some of the other programs you can link to WordStar.

Checking Spelling

The advantage of using SpellStar as your spelling checker is that you do not have to leave WordStar to use it. However, you may find that some of the other spelling-checker programs offer capabilities that make them more attractive. For example, some of them not only find misspelled words but will also offer a list of the most likely correct spellings for you to choose from. Some may include a larger dictionary. Below is a list of some of SpellStar's major competitors and their manufacturers' names and addresses.

SPELLGUARD
Innovative Software
1150 Chestnut Lane
Menlo Park, CA 94025

PROOFREADER
Aspen Software
P. O. Box 339-W
Tijeras, NM 87059

CORRECTOR
SuperSoft
P. O. Box 1628
Champaign, IL 61820

Checking Grammar

You have probably realized that even a spelling-checker program will not find all your errors, because some of them will be properly spelled words in the wrong place in your document. Grammatik can check for double words (such as *to to* in the middle of a sentence) and capitalization at the beginning of a sentence, and can even tell you if you are using cliches or repeating yourself too often.

GRAMMATIK
Aspen Software
P. O. Box 339-W
Tijeras, NM 87059

Finding the Right Word

There is a program that will even find the perfect word for your writing! This program can be accessed while using WordStar, allowing you to ask for a display of all the synonyms for the word you are now using and want to replace. When you have picked one, the program will type it into your document.

RANDOM HOUSE ELECTRONIC THESAURUS
Doctronics
P. O. Box 367
Tijeras, NM 87059

Creating Tables of Contents and Indices

Sometimes the most difficult part of completing a writing project is writing an accurate table of contents or index. Most programs that will write them for you require that you flag each word, phrase, or heading that should appear in the table of contents or index as you enter it in WordStar. When you have completed the document, edited it, and proofread it, you tell the program to create a table of contents or index with the correct page numbers.

DOCUMATE PLUS
Orthocode
P. O. Box 6191
Albany, CA 94706

Orthocode also produces a program called LAWMATE that provides additional indexing capability for attorneys.

Creating Bibliographies and Footnotes

Do you need to develop a bibliography, or are you having trouble keeping track of footnotes as you move text references around in a document? Here are two programs to build and organize a bibliography automatically, or to create and track footnotes so that they are always on the same page as the text reference.

BIBLIOGRAPHY
Digital Marketing
2670 Cherry Lane
Walnut Creek, Ca 94596

FOOTNOTE
Digital Marketing
2670 Cherry Lane
Walnut Creek, CA 94596

Index

Note: Page numbers displayed in regular typeface include a discussion or definition of a topic. Page numbers displayed in **boldface** note locations where a command or operation is used in an application.

The SYBEX Library

INTRODUCTION TO COMPUTERS

DON'T (or How to Care for Your Computer)
by Rodnay Zaks 214 pp., 100 illustr., Ref. 0-065
The correct way to handle and care for all elements of a computer system, including what to do when something doesn't work.

YOUR FIRST COMPUTER
by Rodnay Zaks 258 pp., 150 illustr., Ref. 0-045
The most popular introduction to small computers and their peripherals: what they do and how to buy one.

INTERNATIONAL MICROCOMPUTER DICTIONARY
120 pp., Ref. 0-067
All the definitions and acronyms of microcomputer jargon defined in a handy pocket-size edition. Includes translations of the most popular terms into ten languages.

FROM CHIPS TO SYSTEMS: AN INTRODUCTION TO MICROPROCESSORS
by Rodnay Zaks 552 pp., 400 illustr., Ref. 0-063
A simple and comprehensive introduction to microprocessors from both a hardware and software standpoint: what they are, how they operate, how to assemble them into a complete system.

FOR YOUR APPLE

THE EASY GUIDE TO YOUR APPLE II®
by Joseph Kascmer 160 pp., illustr., Ref. 0-0122
A friendly introduction to using the Apple II, II plus, and the new IIe.

APPLE II® BASIC HANDBOOK
by Douglas Hergert, 144 pp., Ref. 0-115
A complete listing with descriptions and instructive examples of each of the Apple II BASIC keywords and functions. A handy reference guide, organized like a dictionary.

APPLE II® BASIC PROGRAMS IN MINUTES
by Stanley R. Trost 150 pp., illustr., Ref. 0-121
A collection of ready-to-run programs for financial calculations, investment analysis, record keeping, and many more home and office applications. These programs can be entered on your Apple II plus or IIe in minutes!

YOUR FIRST APPLE II® PROGRAM
by Rodnay Zaks 150 pp. illustr., Ref. 0-136
A fully illustrated, easy-to-use introduction to APPLE BASIC programming. Will have the reader programming in a matter of hours.

IBM® PC DOS HANDBOOK

by Richard King 144 pp., illustr., Ref. 0-103

Explains the PC disk operating system, giving the user better control over the system. Get the most out of your PC by adapting its capabilities to your specific needs.

BUSINESS GRAPHICS FOR THE IBM® PC

by Nelson Ford 200 pp., illustr., Ref. 0-124

Ready-to-run programs for creating line graphs, complex illustrative multiple bar graphs, picture graphs, and more. An ideal way to use your PC's business capabilities!

THE IBM® PC CONNECTION

by James W. Coffron 200 pp., illustr., Ref. 0-127

Teaches elementary interfacing and BASIC programming of the IBM PC for connection to external devices and household appliances.

BASIC EXERCISES FOR THE IBM® PERSONAL COMPUTER

by J.P. Lamoitier 252 pp., 90 illustr., Ref. 0-088

Teaches IBM BASIC through actual practice, using graduated exercises drawn from everyday applications.

USEFUL BASIC PROGRAMS FOR THE IBM® PC

by Stanley R. Trost 144 pp., Ref. 0-111

This collection of programs takes full advantage of the interactive capabilities of your IBM Personal Computer. Financial calculations, investment analysis, record keeping, and math practice—made easier on your IBM PC.

FOR YOUR TIMEX/SINCLAIR 1000/ZX81

YOUR TIMEX/SINCLAIR 1000™ AND ZX81™

by Douglas Hergert 159 pp., illustr., Ref. 0-099

This book explains the set-up, operation, and capabilities of the Timex/Sinclair 1000 and ZX81. Includes how to interface peripheral devices, and introduces BASIC programming.

FOR YOUR TRS-80

YOUR COLOR COMPUTER

by Doug Mosher 350 pp., illustr., Ref. 0-097

Patience and humor guide the reader through purchasing, setting up, programming, and using the Radio Shack TRS-80/TDP Series 100 Color Computer. A complete introduction.

THE FOOLPROOF GUIDE TO SCRIPSIT™ WORD PROCESSING

by Jeff Berner 225 pp., illustr., Ref. 0-098

Everything you need to know about SCRIPSIT—from starting out, to mastering document editing. This user-friendly guide is written in plain English, with a touch of wit.

BUSINESS & PROFESSIONAL

COMPUTER POWER FOR YOUR LAW OFFICE
by Daniel Remer 225 pp., Ref. 0-109
How to use computers to reach peak productivity in your law office, simply and inexpensively.

INTRODUCTION TO WORD PROCESSING
by Hal Glatzer 205 pp., 140 illustr., Ref. 0-076
Explains in plain language what a word processor can do, how it improves productivity, how to use a word processor and how to buy one wisely.

INTRODUCTION TO WORDSTAR™
by Arthur Naiman 202 pp., 30 illustr., Ref. 0-077
Makes it easy to learn how to use WordStar, a powerful word processing program for personal computers.

MASTERING VISICALC®
by Douglas Hergert 217 pp., 140 illustr., Ref. 0-090
Explains how to use the VisiCalc "electronic spreadsheet" functions and provides examples of each. Makes using this powerful program simple.

DOING BUSINESS WITH VISICALC®
by Stanley R. Trost 260 pp., Ref. 0-086
Presents accounting and management planning applications—from financial statements to master budgets; from pricing models to investment strategies.

DOING BUSINESS WITH SUPERCALC™
by Stanley R. Trost 248 pp., illustr., Ref. 0-095
Presents accounting and management planning applications—from financial statements to master budgets; from pricing models to investment strategies.

VISICALC® FOR SCIENCE AND ENGINEERING
by Stanley R. Trost & Charles Pomernacki 225 pp., illustr., Ref. 0-096
More than 50 programs for solving technical problems in the science and engineering fields. Applications range from math and statistics to electrical and electronic engineering.

BASIC

YOUR FIRST BASIC PROGRAM
by Rodnay Zaks 150pp. illustr. in color, Ref. 0-129
A "how-to-program" book for the first time computer user, aged 8 to 88.

FIFTY BASIC EXERCISES
by J. P. Lamoitier 232 pp., 90 illustr., Ref. 0-056
Teaches BASIC by actual practice, using graduated exercises drawn from everyday applications. All programs written in Microsoft BASIC.

INSIDE BASIC GAMES
by Richard Mateosian 348 pp., 120 illustr., Ref. 0-055
Teaches interactive BASIC programming through games. Games are written in Microsoft BASIC and can run on the TRS-80, Apple II and PET/CBM.

DOING BUSINESS WITH PASCAL

by Richard Hergert & Douglas Hergert 371 pp., illustr., Ref. 0-091

Practical tips for using Pascal in business programming. Includes design considerations, language extensions, and applications examples.

OTHER LANGUAGES

FORTRAN PROGRAMS FOR SCIENTISTS AND ENGINEERS

by Alan R. Miller 280 pp., 120 illustr., Ref. 0-082

In the "Programs for Scientists and Engineers" series, this book provides specific scientific and engineering application programs written in FORTRAN.

CP/M

THE CP/M® HANDBOOK

by Rodnay Zaks 320 pp., 100 illustr., Ref. 0-048

An indispensable reference and guide to CP/M—the most widely-used operating system for small computers.

MASTERING CP/M®

by Alan R. Miller 398 pp., Ref. 0-068

For advanced CP/M users or systems programmers who want maximum use of the CP/M operating system ... takes up where our *CP/M Handbook* leaves off.

THE BEST OF CP/M® SOFTWARE

by Alan R. Miller 250 pp., illustr., Ref. 0-100

This book reviews tried-and-tested, commercially available software for your CP/M system.

ASSEMBLY LANGUAGE PROGRAMMING

PROGRAMMING THE 6502

by Rodnay Zaks 386 pp., 160 illustr., Ref. 0-046

Assembly language programming for the 6502, from basic concepts to advanced data structures.

PROGRAMMING THE Z80

by Rodnay Zaks 624 pp., 200 illustr., Ref. 0-069

A complete course in programming the Z80 microprocessor and a thorough introduction to assembly language.

PROGRAMMING THE 6809

by Rodnay Zaks and William Labiak 362 pp., 150 illustr., Ref. 0-078

This book explains how to program the 6809 in assembly language. No prior programming knowledge required.

PROGRAMMING THE 8086/8088

by James W. Coffron 300 pp., illustr., Ref. 0-120

This book explains how to program the 8086 and 8088 in asembly language. No prior programming knowledge required.